THE SECOND WORLD WAR IN EUROPE

The Second World War in Europe

S. P. MACKENZIE

LONGMAN
LONDON AND NEW YORK

Addison Wesley Longman Limited,
Edinburgh Gate,
Harlow,
Essex CM20 2JE,
United Kingdom
and Associated Companies throughout the world.

*Published in the United States of America
by Addison Wesley Longman Inc. New York*

First published 1999

ISBN 0 582 32692 3 PPR

Visit Addison Wesley Longman on the world wide web at http://www.awl-he.com

British Library Cataloguing-in-Publication Data
A catalogue record for this book is available from the British Library

Library of Congress Cataloging-in-Publication Data
Mackenzie, S. P.
  The Second World War in Europe / S.P. Mackenzie.
    p.   cm. -- (Seminar studies in history)
  Includes bibliographical references and index.
  ISBN 0 582 32692 3
  1. World War, 1939-1945--Europe. 2. Europe--History--1918-1945.
  I. Title. II. Series.
  D743.M237   1999
  940.53--dc21   98-39608
                                                           CIP

Set by 7 in 10/12 Sabon
Printed in Malaysia, CLP

CONTENTS

AN INTRODUCTION TO THE SERIES

Such is the pace of historical enquiry in the modern world that there is an ever-widening gap between the specialist article or monograph, incorporating the results of current research, and general surveys, which inevitably become out of date. *Seminar Studies in History* are designed to bridge this gap. The series was founded by Patrick Richardson in 1966 and his aim was to cover major themes in British, European and World history. Between 1980 and 1996 Roger Lockyer continued his work, before handing the editorship over to Clive Emsley and Gordon Martel. Clive Emsley is Professor of History at the Open University, while Gordon Martel is Professor of International History at the University of Northern British Columbia, Canada and Senior Research Fellow at De Montfort University.

All the books are written by experts in their field who are not only familiar with the latest research but have often contributed to it. They are frequently revised, in order to take account of new information and interpretations. They provide a selection of documents to illustrate major themes and provoke discussion, and also a guide to further reading. The aim of *Seminar Studies* is to clarify complex issues without over-simplifying them, and to stimulate readers into deepening their knowledge and understanding of major themes and topics.

LIST OF MAPS

NOTE ON REFERENCING SYSTEM

Readers should note that numbers in square brackets [5] refer them to the corresponding entry in the Bibliography at the end of the book (specific page numbers are given in italics). A number in square brackets preceded by *Doc.* [*Doc. 5*] refers readers to the corresponding item in the Documents section which follows the main text. Words and abbreviations asterisked at first occurrence are defined in the Glossary, and named individuals asterisked at first occurrence are described in the Guide to Characters.

PREFACE

Matching the scale of destruction and upheaval generated by the war itself, the published literature on the Second World War is gargantuan. Indeed, with so much material to draw upon, those historians who attempted to write or compile general histories of the war to mark the fiftieth anniversary tended to produce truly massive tomes [7, 9, 15]. There are, to be sure, a few recent overviews of more manageable proportions [11, 12, 14], but there is little in the way of an introduction to the subject for the younger generations for whom World War II is *terra incognita*. Hence this little book.

ACKNOWLEDGEMENTS

The publishers would like to thank the following for permission to reproduce copyright material: Cassell Plc for permission to include a redrawn version of the map 'The Battle of the Atlantic' from *History of the Second World War* by B H Liddell Hart, pp. 372–3, 1970; HarperCollins Publishers Ltd for tables 31, 32 and 34 from *The Rise and Fall of the Great Powers* by Paul Kennedy pp. 430 and 455 and an extract from Diary of a German Soldier in *Battle for Stalingrad* by V Chuikov pp. 253–4; Hutchison for permission to include amended versions of the maps 'The Battle of France', p. 75, 'Barbarossa', p. 183, 'The Italian Campaign', p. 355, 'The Normandy Breakout', p. 406 and 'The Red Army Moves West', p. 503, from *The Second World War* by John Keegan, 1989.

Whilst every effort has been made to trace the owners of copyright material, in a few cases this has proved to be problematic and so we take this opportunity to offer our apologies to any copyright holders whose rights we may have unwittingly infringed.

PART ONE: BACKGROUND

1 THE ROAD TO WAR

THE ORIGINS OF THE WAR

The origins of the Second World War continue to generate debate among historians. However, though interpretations and emphases may differ, Germany is always at the centre of efforts to explore the origins of World War II [42].

That Germany should be centre stage is not surprising. Without control of a powerful state, Adolf Hitler* would have been a marginal figure; and in a broad sense the Second World War in Europe was about whether or not Germany, united since the 1870s and possessed of enormous industrial potential, should become the dominant power on the Continent. That was the central issue underlying the outbreak of World War I in 1914, and despite the defeat of Imperial Germany in 1918, it remained unresolved in the interwar years. The peace treaty imposed by the Allies at Versailles in 1919, though harsh in some respects – loss of border territories to neighbouring states, significant reparation demands, and the reduction of the armed forces to a size and scale capable only of maintaining order at home – left the German state and its economy pretty much intact.

Under the Weimar Republic efforts were made to restore German power and prestige through evading or undermining the restrictions imposed on German freedom of action at Versailles. Confrontation in the immediate postwar years, when Germany was still prostrate, achieved little. But by the mid-1920s a more subtle yet pragmatic approach to diplomacy yielded concrete results. Patiently exploiting British guilt over Versailles (arising from the growing belief that no single state had borne overall responsibility for war in 1914) and French desires for a peaceful resolution to Franco-German confrontation, Gustav Stresemann and others negotiated a series of agreements and treaties which substantially altered the balance of power to German advantage. Reparations were progressively scaled back through the Dawes Plan (1924) and the Young Plan (1929), and

Germany's position as a diplomatic – though not military – equal among nations was restored through the Locarno Treaties of 1925 and other agreements.

This evolutionary process came to an abrupt end with the onset of the Great Depression and the rise of the Nazis in the early 1930s. Though reparations became a moot point as the international economy collapsed, mass unemployment stimulated support for extremists and created deadlock in efforts at the League of Nations to ameliorate the military restrictions imposed on Germany. Moreover, once Hitler came to power in 1933 his ideology of struggle and determination to restore German might – and ultimately reverse the verdict of 1918 – propelled the European balance of power towards revolutionary rather than evolutionary change. Though it is possible to imagine other regimes in Germany continuing to pursue alterations in the *status quo*, Hitler, as Führer* of the new Third Reich, forced the pace with such aggressive militancy that another European war became increasingly likely, though not necessarily inevitable, as the decade wore on.

With little in the way of a coherent strategy to draw upon but filled with a burning desire to confront and overwhelm, Hitler sought to expand the German armed forces as fast as possible. At first rearmament was kept more or less secret, but in March 1935 the disarmament clauses of the Versailles Treaty were publicly repudiated. The nascent *Luftwaffe** was unveiled and conscription introduced as a means of building up the 100,000-man army allowed by the Treaty of Versailles into a *Wehrmacht** of well over 500,000 men. In renouncing the Versailles disarmament clauses Hitler had issued his first overt challenge to Germany's former enemies. How they reacted then, and in subsequent crises generated by Hitler's actions, would pave the road to war.

The paramount security concern within the Third Republic of France was to avoid isolation when dealing with Germany, which meant working in concert with the Allies. With the United States having withdrawn from European security arrangements in 1919, France by the mid-1930s was left with a series of alliances with small powers in Eastern Europe dating from the 1920s, a recently concluded but untested mutual assistance pact with the Soviet Union (1935), and the conviction that the one other former ally and Great Power in the West – Britain – must not be alienated. French reliance on British goodwill meant in turn that the British government could take the lead in determining how to respond to Hitler [56].

For centuries one of the main strategic interests of British governments had been to prevent any single Great Power from achieving hegemony on the Continent. Shoring up the balance of power in Europe through diplomatic and, if necessary, armed force, guarded against the rise of a single power strong enough to threaten the British Isles. In essence this was why Britain had gone to war against Imperial Germany in 1914. By the 1930s, however, strategic realities were clouded by other considerations.

The First World War had been a traumatic and costly experience for Britain. The economy had been exhausted and over 730,000 soldiers killed (and a much larger number wounded). This in turn generated widespread revulsion against war as an instrument of policy, a pacifistic mood which found strength from the popular view that an unstable military-diplomatic system rather than the aggressiveness of the Central Powers had driven Europe into the abyss in 1914. This in turn promoted guilt over the punitive nature of the Treaty of Versailles. Even in the 1920s and early 1930s, with Germany still very much the underdog, British governments had been eager to avoid confrontation. Once Hitler began to rearm Germany in the second half of the 1930s and make threats, the desire to negotiate rather than confront took on more urgency. A sense that Hitler might have legitimate grievances stemming from Versailles, coupled with memories of bloody trench warfare as well as fears of an aerial Armageddon (mass destruction of British cities by the rapidly expanding German air force), combined to make Appeasement appear the natural course to follow.

Appeasement, as pursued rather lazily by the government of Stanley Baldwin and much more actively by his successor Neville Chamberlain,* was based on the assumption that Hitler, however bellicose his talk, was ultimately interested in peaceful rather than forceful revision of territorial and other issues arising from Versailles. This was a great mistake. Though he possessed no master plan and was in many respects an opportunist improvisor lacking a coherent strategic vision, the Führer firmly believed in the necessity of armed struggle between nations and was more than willing to risk war to achieve complete dominance in Central Europe and liberate more *Lebensraum* (living space) for the German people in general. Hitler was, however, quite able to play upon British hopes and fears through a judicious mixture of claims of peaceful intent and threats of warlike action [48, 50].

When open German rearmament began in 1935, and when Hitler sent troops into the Rhineland in March 1936 (the area between the Rhine and French border which had been demilitarized in 1919), the initial shock soon gave way to rationalization and optimistic hopes for the future in London. Germany had every right to behave as a sovereign state by building an army and placing troops anywhere it liked within its borders. Moreover, had not Hitler expressed eagerness to negotiate a peaceful settlement of Germany's grievances?

There were, to be sure, moments of pragmatism in relation to latent German aggression in the mid-1930s. In March 1935, rearmament slowly began to get under way. In the following month Britain and France had begun negotiating with Mussolini* in an attempt to present a united diplomatic front against Hitler. This attempt at *de facto* coalition building, however, quickly collapsed. A short-sighted Anglo-German agreement on naval limits in June 1935, made without consulting Paris, suggested a distinct lack of enthusiasm for an Anglo-French entente. Mussolini's full-scale invasion of Abyssinia, launched in October 1935, forced both Britain and France to vote for sanctions against Italy in the League of Nations. This put paid to the idea of a united front and propelled Mussolini into overtly aligning with Germany through the so-called Rome-Berlin Axis* announced in November 1936 [51].

Appeasement, in any case, remained the dominant theme in British diplomacy. For a time efforts focused on possible colonial concessions; but by 1938 it was clear that Hitler's true interests lay in Central Europe.

In March of that year Hitler sent troops to Vienna in a bloodless *coup* that led to the incorporation of Austria (*Anschluss*) into the German Reich. Protests were lodged against yet another breach of the Versailles Treaty (Germany and Austria were supposed to remain independent of one another), but as many Austrians appeared to be happy to be as one with their German cousins, nothing of any consequence was done.

Almost at once, however, a new crisis began to build up. Germans living in the Sudetenland, the border region of Czechoslovakia next to the Reich, were encouraged to demand union with the Fatherland, and Hitler began to threaten a forceful solution to the issue. France was bound by treaty to defend Czechoslovakia, and, via the 1935 treaty, the Soviet Union would also be drawn in if war began. By September 1938, with Hitler making increasingly bellicose threats to solve the Sudeten problem by force if his demands were not met at once and in full, the likelihood of war seemed very real. Chamberlain and his Cabinet colleagues, however, worried about the prospect of air attack and still hoped that Appeasement could work. The Sudetenlanders were mostly German and their incorporation into Czechoslovakia, rather than Germany or Austria, was yet another consequence of the Treaty of Versailles. Hence Britain, after some initial hesitation, once again shied away from the threat of force. The Czechs, abandoned by their French ally (which in turn made null and void the possibility of Soviet support), were forced by Chamberlain to agree to cede the Sudetenland on Hitler's terms at the Munich Conference at the end of September 1938 [55].

Thus far Hitler had gambled and won. His generals, concerned that the armed forces were not really ready for war either in 1936 or even 1938, were overruled in the expectation that the Western Powers would not fight when push came to shove (though signs of depression after Munich suggest that at some level Hitler would have preferred a war in any event). In 1939, however, events assumed a new aspect.

Hitler continued to behave aggressively, negating Chamberlain's hope that at Munich he had achieved 'peace in our time'. In March of 1939 Hitler sent troops into Prague. From his perspective, this was simply rounding off what had been achieved at Munich, incorporating the remnants of a state that had been rendered broken and helpless by the events of September 1938. In London, however, it was the first truly unambiguous signal that Hitler was bent on far more than righting the wrongs of Versailles: these were not Germans who were being absorbed into the Reich. Rearmament in Britain was already accelerating, and in March and April 1939 the Chamberlain government, once again compelling France to move in tandem, guaranteed the independence of a number of the smaller states in Central Europe that might come under German threat – not least Poland, which seemed to be next on Hitler's list.

Appeasement had been replaced, belatedly, by an attempt at containment. This effort, however, was a case of too little too late. The Polish government took a tough line, flatly refusing Hitler's demand for the incorporation of the free city of Danzig and a land route across the Polish corridor between East Prussia and Germany proper. After Munich, however, Hitler had every reason to believe Britain and France would back down at the last moment and abandon Poland if Germany threatened or used force. Moreover, the alliances the British and French were making were not with the Great Powers. Mussolini and the democracies remained estranged, and – more importantly – Stalin was extremely wary of Anglo-French efforts to conclude an alliance.

The Munich agreement had made Stalin* suspect that capitalist Britain and France were more interested in turning Hitler's attention east than in forming a united front with the USSR. This suspicion was apparently confirmed by the rather half-hearted nature of the Western efforts to conclude a military alliance with the Soviet Union once Appeasement had been abandoned in 1939. In truth, Chamberlain found the idea of an alliance with communist Russia highly distasteful, and there were doubts among the military chiefs in both London and Paris about the readiness of the Red Army for war after the purging of the officer corps in 1937–38. When Hitler suddenly began to push for a *rapprochement* between Germany and Russia in August 1939, chiefly directed against Poland, Stalin was ready to do business [52].

The signing of the Nazi-Soviet Pact on 23 August 1939 made Hitler more certain than ever that when he moved against Poland, the British and French, deprived of their potential Great Power ally, would acquiesce. Despite the shock of the pact, however, public and government opinion in Britain and, perhaps to a lesser extent, France, was against further appeasement. Hitler had shown his true colours, and had to be stopped. Hence when German forces moved against Poland at the beginning of September 1939, Hitler's bluff was called and war declared. The Second World War in Europe had begun [*Doc. 1*] [54].

PREPARING FOR WAR

As the likelihood of war increased in the 1930s, all the major European states had begun rearmament programmes. Paradoxically, however, none of them – not even Germany – was in a state of full readiness when war came.

Given Hitler's dedication to building up the German armed forces in the 1930s (devoting almost a quarter of the national income to the task in 1937 alone) and the stunning German victories in the early years of the war, it is tempting to assume that the *Wehrmacht* (the German armed forces, particularly the army) possessed a marked superiority over its rivals in terms of strength and equipment. This was not, in fact, the case. Though rearmament had proceeded at a breakneck pace in Germany, the build-up of the armed forces was by no means complete by the time war broke out.

The expansion of the German surface fleet was not due to be completed until the mid-1940s, leaving the handful of heavy ships in the *Kriegsmarine** (German navy) incapable of mounting a direct challenge to its British rival, the Royal Navy. After mobilization of reserves on the outbreak of war the German army possessed over 3,700,000 men organized into 103 divisions, including six of the new Panzer (armoured) divisions, which together deployed nearly 3,000 tanks. Beneath these impressive figures, however, lay weaknesses.

Table 1 War Potential of the Great Powers, *c.* 1937.

State	Population (millions)	National income ($ billions)	Percentage of income spent on defence	Relative war potential
USA	129	68	1.5%	41.7%
Germany	68	17	23.5%	14.4%
USSR	167	19	26.4%	14.0%
UK	47	22	5.7%	10.2%
France	41	10	9.1%	4.2%
Japan	70	4	28.2%	3.5%
Italy	43	6	14.5%	2.5%

The huge expansion of the army had meant that many of the units called up when war began lacked training, enough specialists, and, worse still, adequate equipment. There was not enough motor transport to go around, and even the best-equipped infantry divisions had to rely heavily on horses. The more modern types of gun were in short supply for both artillery and infantry units, and even the vaunted Panzer divisions were seriously short of medium and heavy tanks and armoured transports for their accompanying support troops. Almost one third of the mobilized army, indeed, could only be employed as a replacement pool out of harm's way. In terms of weapons, equipment, and numbers, the German army possessed nothing that approached an overwhelming superiority over the combined French and British armies. Only the *Luftwaffe*, with over 2,500 operational aircraft of modern design, possessed a clear numerical advantage over Germany's opponents [45].

What would really distinguish the *Wehrmacht* from its adversaries in the early years of the war, however, was its tactical and operational proficiency. Drawing on the professional legacy of the old Imperial Army and the innovations pioneered by the 1920s *Reichswehr* (the army of the Weimar Republic), staff work and planning for campaigns was of very high order, air and ground forces were well integrated, and officers at all levels were trained to be flexible and take the initiative. Hitler, as head of the armed forces since 1938, determined strategy (usually of a highly aggressive nature). It was the job of army planners and field commanders to turn his directives into operational realities: something for which, even with limited means, they and the men under them were well suited. Success would not come as the result of a revolutionary new way of war labelled *Blitzkrieg** by the Allies, but rather out of a willingness to integrate new weapons such as tanks and aeroplanes into traditional operational thinking; the result being an evolutionary, rather than revolutionary, process whose main effect was to speed up the pace of what were, in some ways, quite traditional battles of encirclement [43].

When the war began Germany's main enemy was France. In 1939 the French possessed a mobilized army of just under 5 million men organized in fifty-six infantry divisions, seven motorized infantry divisions, three light mechanized divisions, and (by 1940) three armoured divisions. The French also possessed over 3,000 tanks, many of high quality. Moreover, the French army was sheltered in and behind the impressive Maginot Line,* a series of deep fortifications along the Franco-German frontier built in the 1930s. Like the *Wehrmacht,* however, the French armed forces were in certain respects – some of them crucial – unready for war.

Though the French navy was strong, the poorly organized and badly equipped air force was weak. Even after nine months of war the French air force still possessed only a thousand or so modern aircraft. As for the army, there were serious shortages of anti-aircraft and anti-tank guns, as well as radios, motor vehicles, and ammunition of all kinds. As a result of a slow and somewhat incoherent rearmament effort in the 1930s (France had spent only 9.1 per cent of its 1937 national income on defence), much French equipment remained obsolescent.

However, it was the command system and attitude of mind of the French land and air force commanders that most seriously weakened the French capacity to fight effectively when war came. Though efforts had been made to adapt to changing military technology, the French army was, in essence, organized for a 1914 to 1918-style war. Campaigns along continuous fronts would involve meticulous planning, methodical artillery preparation, slow infantry advances supported by tanks, all under rigid top-down control. The effect of air support, unit initiative, and above all the potential speed and power of concentrated armour, was not properly appreciated [41, 44].

Great Britain, which would end up at war with Germany longer than any other power, had also been rearming (in 1937 spending about 5 per cent of national income on defence) and also possessed strengths and weaknesses in 1939. The Royal Navy, though saddled with many ageing ships, was still more than a match for the surface units of the *Kriegsmarine.* With help from the powerful French navy, possible intervention by the Italian navy in the Mediterranean could also be countered successfully. There were doubts, however, about what would happen if Britain found itself at war with Japan as well. The Royal Air Force (RAF*), the chief beneficiary of the rearmament effort of the latter 1930s, possessed over 1,900 aircraft of varying quality. Of these, 920 mostly obsolescent bombers and 130 front-line fighters would be dispatched to assist France. Strategic bombing and more recently fighter defence of the home islands had been the focus of attention within the prewar RAF, which meant little thought or training had been devoted to the issue of air assistance for ground operations.

The British army, starved of funds through much of the inter-war period and mustering only 897,000 men when war broke out, immediately sent 152,000 men to France to form the nucleus of the British Expeditionary Force (BEF).* In the last years of peace the infantry component of the British army had been motorized (putting it ahead of all other armies in this respect), but there were deficiencies in training and equipment, particularly in anti-tank and anti-aircraft artillery and infantry support weapons. As for the 640 or so British tanks, they were organized along traditional lines: the majority were light tanks to be used in place of horse cavalry for reconnaissance, while heavier models were to be used mostly in support of the infantry. Though the British army had been a pioneer experimenting with large mechanized formations in the early 1930s, it was only in 1940 that its first armoured division was hastily cobbled together from smaller units. British generals, like their French counterparts, mostly anticipated a war centering on slow build-ups and advances, continuous fronts, and methodical infantry and artillery actions.

In short, while nobody was ready for war in 1939, and although the war potential of Britain and France when combined roughly equalled that of Germany, there were significant differences between the two sides. In northeastern France and the Low Countries, where both sides expected the main clash of arms to take place, the German and Allied land and air forces began to prepare to fight each other at a very different tempo.

As for the powers that were still neutral in 1939 – Italy, the Soviet Union, and, more distantly, the United States – their armed forces were also in a state of transition. In each case entry into the war (in June 1940, June 1941, and December 1941 respectively) would reveal serious weaknesses.

Fascist Italy had spent approximately 14.5 per cent of its national income on defence in 1937, a relatively high figure which nevertheless could not mask the fact that industrial and raw material weaknesses still made Italy the weakest of the Great Powers. Like the French fleet that it was built to oppose in the Mediterranean, the Italian navy possessed a wide variety of modern ships with the exception of aircraft carriers. Many of the aeroplanes of the Italian *Regia Aeronautica*,* however, though first-rate in the mid-1930s, were approaching obsolescence by the time Mussolini decided to come in on what he thought was the winning side. As for the tradition-bound Italian army, of its seventy-three divisions only three were armoured and another three motorized when war with the Allies broke out. In terms of equipment, there were shortages of radios, anti-aircraft and anti-tank guns, and Italian tanks were uniformly weak and underpowered [53].

The Soviet Union, in contrast, possessed both ample natural resources and a large and secure arms industry as a result of the industrialization drives of the 1930s. The Red Army was truly massive: there were 5.37 million men under arms even before mobilization. Its sixty-one armoured divisions and thirty-one motorized divisions possessed between them 20,000 tanks (mostly obsolete or obsolescent by 1941, but also as many as 2,000 of the most modern design in the world). The air force deployed about 10,000 aircraft, over 2,500 of them quite modern types. Even the Soviet navy, hitherto neglected, was expanding as a result of a large shipbuilding programme initiated in 1938.

The Soviet armed forces, however, and in particular the all-important Red Army, was in fact dangerously weak in the years preceding 1941. Its most senior and innovative generals had been swept away in the latter 1930s during the Great Purge, and their replacements, though considered politically reliable by Stalin, were dangerously lacking in knowledge and initiative. Even after the very poor performance of the Red Army in the Winter War of 1939-40 against Finland brought about some operational and other reforms, the Soviet armed forces, partly as a result of Stalin's personal preferences, were not prepared to fight a *Blitzkrieg* in 1941.

The United States, meanwhile, had slowly begun to adjust in the late 1930s and the first years of war to the possibility that Americans might once more have to fight in Europe. In 1937 a mere 1.5 per cent of national income had been spent on the armed forces. The following year, however, the US navy – growing since 1933 – began a shipbuilding programme that by 1940 (when the programme was expanded further still) was already producing some of the modern and diverse types of ship that would help win the war (notably aircraft carriers).

In 1939 the air corps (soon to be labeled USAAF (United States Army Air Forces)) also received clearance to expand to a total force of 5,300 aircraft – over 3,200 to be of modern design. The US army, meanwhile, only began to expand seriously in 1940 after the fall of France, mustering 1.2 million ill-trained men as a result of the first peacetime draft. Though military doctrine stressed firepower, the US army was very weak in terms of equipment, possessing only a scratch armoured force of light vehicles in 1940 and a single combat-ready infantry division when war broke out in 1941. Plans, however, were already being laid in September 1941 for an expansion in both men and material that would make the US army among the largest and the most lavishly equipped in the world by 1944 [47].

PART TWO: THE SECOND WORLD WAR

2   THE FLOW OF *BLITZKRIEG*, 1939–42

CAMPAIGNS EAST AND WEST, 1939–40

The Fall of Poland

Once it became clear in September 1939 that Britain and France as allies would not abandon Poland to its fate, it became imperative for the German army to defeat the Poles as quickly as possible. With the bulk of German forces committed in the east, Germany's western border was vulnerable to attack; if the campaign in Poland dragged on too long, the mobilized French army would be in a position to launch an offensive into Germany against only light opposition. The German public was undoubtedly apprehensive [*Doc. 2*].

The odds against long-term Polish survival, however, were slim. The Polish air force was both numerically and technically inferior to the *Luftwaffe*, while the large Polish army lacked modern heavy weapons and relied heavily on cavalry to make up for a critical short-age of armoured fighting vehicles. However, the speed with which the Poles were defeated by the Germans – a matter of weeks – was in part due to strategic errors committed by Hitler's adversaries.

Hoping to protect the more populous and economically vital west-ern portion of Poland, the Polish staff adopted a strategy of forward defence, with Poland's armies grouped along the border regions rather than (as might have been more prudent) establishing a defence in depth anchored on the Vistula river line. Spreading Polish forces along the border all the way from the Baltic Sea to the Carpathian Moun-tains played into enemy hands, since the German plan of campaign involved mounting a series of large pincer drives through Polish defences, the aim being to encircle and destroy the main Polish forces before moving on Warsaw. With the *Luftwaffe* in command of the skies and German motorized and armoured elements able to advance at great speed, most of the slow-moving Polish armies were encircled and effectively destroyed within two weeks of the outbreak of war. A counterstroke was attempted by retreating Polish forces on 9 September but after a few days this was checked and the German advance continued towards Warsaw.

The third week of war sealed Poland's fate. In prewar staff talks the French had promised to launch a spoiling offensive in the west fifteen days into the war. Instead of a French offensive that would draw off German forces however, the Poles were faced with another adversary. The promised French offensive never materialized, and on 17 September the Red Army invaded from the east, as planned for in a secret protocol to the Nazi–Soviet Pact. Bombed from the air and itself encircled by German ground forces, Warsaw capitulated on 27 September. At relatively modest cost (around 45,000 Germans killed, wounded or missing as against about 200,000 Polish casualties), the *Wehrmacht* had in the course of a few weeks utterly defeated its adversary. Soviet intervention only brought a foregone conclusion a few days nearer, organized resistance ceasing on 5 October [65].

Strategy and the Phoney War

In the aftermath of Poland's defeat an uneasy calm ensued between Germany on the one hand and Britain and France on the other. Armies faced one another behind frontier defences, but apart from occasional patrolling and sparring in the air, combat in late 1939 and the first months of 1940 was confined to the sea. This did not mean, however, that either side was idle: indeed, both sides were laying plans for final victory.

The Allies were preparing for an extended struggle. In London, if not always in Paris, the expectation was that time was on the Allies' side. A naval blockade in combination with a future bombing campaign would slowly starve the German war economy. Meanwhile Britain and France would mobilize their superior economic resources, and either Hitler would be overthrown from within or a land invasion of Germany would take place. Just how vulnerable Germany was to this strategy remains unclear, but there is no doubt that Hitler himself thought that the *Wehrmacht* needed to take the initiative and defeat its enemies decisively rather than engage in a drawn-out war of attrition. It was fairly obvious, therefore, that the next clash of arms would involve a German offensive in the west.

With the Maginot Line providing an effective barrier against a major German breakthrough along most of the Franco–German border, the most likely avenue for a German advance was through neutral Belgium and Luxembourg. Both sides, indeed, initially planned for such a move. The initial German plans for the offensive, first scheduled to begin as early as November 1939 but repeatedly postponed into the spring of 1940, foresaw the main action occurring in the north where Army Group B would push westward into Belgium and then southward in an enveloping manoeuvre. General Maurice Gamelin,* meanwhile, supreme commander of both the French forces and the Expeditionary Force under General Lord Gort,* planned to defeat this expected move by pushing the BEF and the best trained and more mobile units of the French army northeast to the Dyle river as soon as Belgian neutrality had been violated by the enemy; the aim being to meet and halt the German offensive as far from the French frontier as possible.

Given that, by May 1940, the forces deployed by each side were roughly equal in overall strength – except in the air where the *Luftwaffe* was considerably stronger than the French air force and the RAF units stationed in France – it is possible that had the German High Command employed its original plan, the German offensive in the west might have been brought to a halt in the north. As it was, however, General Karl von Rundstedt, commanding Army Group A, with the help of his Chief of Staff, General Erich von Manstein,* was able to persuade the high command as well as Hitler that the main German effort ought to be shifted southward. While Army Group B occupied the Allies to the north, seven Panzer divisions and the bulk of the infantry assigned to Army Group A would thrust through the hilly and wooded country around Sedan, which had been left unprotected by the Maginot Line. Once a breakthrough had occurred, the Panzer divisions would race for the Channel coast. This new approach was a gamble, since the Panzer divisions would be exposed on their flanks until the slower-moving infantry and other formations caught up. If it worked, however, this plan would mean the main British and French field forces would be trapped and rendered ineffective, caught between two German army groups to the north and south, cut off from their lines of communication and unable to retreat [*Doc. 3*]. Before the armies and their plans could be tested in the west, however, the future of Scandinavia came into question.

Scandinavian Interlude

Stalin, anxious to safeguard the USSR's Baltic flank from possible future attack, made territorial demands on Helsinki in the aftermath of the partition of Poland that the Finns found impossible to accept. In October 1939 the Red Army tried on a broad front to take by force what diplomacy had failed to achieve. Despite a great disparity in men and equipment, the Finnish army was able to hold off the large but badly led Soviet offensives over the winter months. Only in March 1940, in the face of new concentrated Red Army offensives, did Helsinki throw in the towel and accede to Stalin's (now extended) territorial demands [63].

Meanwhile, the weaknesses of the post-purge Red Army had been exposed for all the world to see. Its abysmal performance against tiny Finland doubtless encouraged Hitler when his thoughts turned towards invasion some months later. Events in Finland also influenced events that would produce the first clash of arms between the Allies and Germany since the fall of Poland.

During the months of the so-called phoney war the French government under Premier Edouard Daladier* and then Paul Reynaud,* as well as Gamelin and others in the French High Command, grew increasingly worried that the blockade strategy would not work as things stood. Germany was receiving too much aid in the way of oil, wheat, and raw materials from the Soviet Union, while its iron industry needs were being met by purchasing ore from Sweden which was shipped down the Norwegian coast. The British were cool to the French idea of directly or indirectly attacking the Soviet Union on the pretext of helping Finland; but agreed that something should be done to stop the iron ore flow to Germany from Scandinavia. Initially, the hope was to send troops to occupy northern Norway and Sweden under the pretext of aiding the Finns in their resistance to Soviet territorial demands; when the Finns gave up in March 1940, the plan changed to mining Norwegian territorial waters and sending an expeditionary force to Norway as soon as Hitler retaliated with small-scale attacks in Scandinavia. Unfortunately the enemy had already anticipated an Allied move in Norway and moved to pre-empt it with a full-scale invasion.

Denmark was quickly and bloodlessly occupied by German forces while German naval units disembarked assault troops at key points along the Norwegian coast beginning on 9 April. The Norwegian phase of the operation did not go entirely according to plan, with the German navy in particular suffering heavy losses. But by the time British and French units arrived on the scene to aid the Norwegian army – a full-scale enemy invasion having been dismissed as impossible because of the risks involved to the small German fleet – the Germans were already in place. Only in the far north at Narvik did the British forces achieve a firm foothold by late May; but by this time the Battle of France was going badly for the Allies and Norway had to be abandoned in early June [61].

The Battle of France

When the first German units moved westward on 10 May 1940 into Holland, Belgium and Luxembourg, it looked as if Gamelin had been correct in anticipating the enemy's main thrust. The bulk of the BEF and the French 7th and 1st armies moved northeast, as planned, to co-operate with the underequipped Belgian and Dutch armies. But they quickly felt the weight of superior German airpower and the two Panzer and twenty-seven infantry divisions of German Army Group B.

Meanwhile, on 13 May 1940, the main German attack by Army Group A (forty-four divisions) began to the south. Seven Panzer divisions with ample air support struck at the relatively weak French 9th and 2nd armies, reaching and crossing the Meuse river and then breaking out to the west within a matter of days [58].

It was at this point, as Gamelin and his subordinates sought to respond to this unexpected drive, that the weakness of the Allied air forces and the slowness and confusion of the command and control system of the ground forces made itself felt. Efforts during 13 to 16 May to move three French armoured divisions held in reserve into a position to attack the German flanks collapsed in a muddle of air attacks, conflicting orders and inadequate logistical arrangements. The Panzers raced on, and by 20 May had reached the sea.

The only hope for the Allied forces was to launch a major counter-stroke by forces north and south of the German corridor against the exposed flanks of the German line of advance before slower German forces could move up to consolidate the gains made. Though an obvious move in theory, and ordered on several occasions in the third and fourth weeks of May, it proved impossible for the Allied commanders to organize effectively. German command of the skies in combination with the lack of combined arms in the remaining British and French tank formations, along with a crisis of morale in the French High Command (which the replacement of Gamelin by General Maxime Weygand* did little to counteract), meant that Allied counterattacks were weak and unco-ordinated. Though they caused momentary alarm to the German High Command, hastily mounted attacks by the newly formed French 4th armoured division and then by a British tank brigade at Arras in the fourth week of May, achieved initial success but foundered for want of sufficient infantry and artillery support. With Army Group B continuing to advance and Belgian resistance collapsing, all subsequent efforts to mount a co-ordinated offensive from north and south foundered.

Map 1. *The Battle of France, 1940*
Source: *The Second World War*, John Keegan, Hutchinson, London, 1989,
p. 75

By the last week of May the BEF and the remains of the French 1st
army were pinned up against the coast around Dunkirk, and on 26
May orders were given to prepare to evacuate as many men as possible
by sea. A certain amount of uncertainty in the German High Com-

mand (OKW*) over which German units should be primarily responsible for eradicating the Dunkirk pocket, combined with too much reliance on the *Luftwaffe* (whose bombing could be partially countered by fighters operating from bases across the English Channel) meant that between 27 May and 4 June 338,000 men (140,000 of them French) were successfully taken off by boat from Dunkirk. The 'Miracle of Dunkirk', however, did nothing to alter the fact that France was on the verge of defeat [57].

Against ninety-five German divisions, including all ten Panzer divisions, now preparing to sweep south in June, General Weygand could only deploy the remnants of forty-five divisions, only three of which were mobile. The outcome of the battle fought between 5 and 9 June along the line of the Somme and Aisne rivers was a foregone conclusion, and once more the Panzers raced forward.

On 14 June, Paris, now an open city, was occupied by the Germans. For a time it seemed as if the French government might carry on the fight from abroad; but on 16 June 1940 the generals and politicians who wanted an end to it all won out over Reynaud and other resisters; and a new leader, Marshal Philippe Pétain*, the ageing hero of the First World War, determined to bring both the war and the 'decadent' republic to an end, sought and obtained German terms for an armistice that was signed on 21 June. The Germans continued to occupy and later exploit the northern part of the country, while in the south a new authoritarian regime was created by Pétain at Vichy* which in coming years would seek to promote French interests by currying favour with the new masters of Europe.

The Battle of Britain

The Battle of France was over; but what of Britain? Chamberlain had been replaced by Winston Churchill* on 10 May as prime minister as a result of the Norway fiasco. Once the BEF had been evacuated, Churchill, with considerable public support, made it clear that Britain would fight on [*Doc. 4*]. German peace feelers were rejected, and the deadly earnestness of British determination demonstrated to friend and foe alike when on 3 July 1940, in order to make absolutely sure the French fleet did not fall into German hands, ships of the Royal Navy bombarded and disabled many of the main units of their former ally's navy that were riding at anchor at Mers-el-Kébir, North Africa (an action which permanently soured relations with Vichy France) [59].

Strategies to win the war now gave way in London to a struggle for survival. A German invasion attempt seemed all but inevitable some time before the onset of winter.

On 16 July, Hitler had indeed issued orders to the army and navy to begin planning for a cross-Channel attack to take place in the early autumn. But it was clear to both sides that the success of any such attempt would depend on control of the skies. Whether or not Britain was invaded would depend on whether the *Luftwaffe* could wear down the RAF to the point where it could not protect the ships of the Royal Navy trying to stop an invasion, nor seriously interfere with German vessels crossing the Channel.

The outcome of the air campaign over southern England in the late summer and autumn of 1940, which became known as the Battle of Britain, was not a foregone conclusion. The *Luftwaffe* of Hermann Goering* began the battle with 1,260 twin-engine medium bombers, 320 dive bombers, 280 twin-engined fighters, and 800 of the excellent single-engine Bf-109s.* RAF Fighter Command,* meanwhile, under the direction of Air Chief Marshal Sir Hugh Dowding,* could deploy under 900 single-engine Spitfire* and Hurricane* fighters, the latter inferior to the Bf-109. Bearing in mind that the German aim was to wear down the RAF on the ground through bombing as well as shooting down enemy fighters in the air, the numerical odds seemed to favour the *Luftwaffe*.

The British did, however, have a few advantages of their own. Fighter Command possessed an excellent early warning and command and control system. The key to this system was a relatively new invention, a radio locating device, better known as radar.* By 1939, a chain of radar stations had been established along the south coast of England that could give enough warning of approaching enemy formations to allow for RAF fighter squadrons to be despatched to intercept them – hopefully before they struck their targets. In addition, British fighters could spend more time aloft over southern England than their adversaries coming across the Channel, and RAF pilots who were forced to bail out generally lived to fight another day (whereas *Luftwaffe* aircrew became prisoners).

The opening round of the battle occurred over the Channel with attacks on British shipping in July. Then in mid-August 1940 the main assault began with bombing attacks on airfields in southern England. *Luftwaffe* losses were disproportionately heavy until the ratio of fighters to bombers was increased in late August. With this, the strain on the RAF began to tell. More German aircraft were being shot down than British aircraft, and British fighters were being produced faster than they were being destroyed; but a serious RAF pilot shortage was developing by early September (231 pilots killed or wounded as against half that number coming from training units between 24 August and 6 September) and serious damage was being done to airfields in southern England. If continued, this battle of attrition might have led to the *Luftwaffe* gaining command of the air over the Channel and southern England. As it was, however, partly as retaliation for a British raid on Berlin and partly in order to draw out what was thought to be the last of the RAF's reserves north of London, the *Luftwaffe* switched to mass daylight attacks on London which began on 7 September. This proved to be a major tactical error. RAF stations were given time to recover, while a single major target fairly far inland made it easier for the RAF to marshal large numbers of fighters to intercept. After 7 September, German losses climbed significantly, the *Luftwaffe* losing 175 aircraft by 15 September. With aircraft and crews not being replaced at the rate they were being lost, the *Luftwaffe* was being significantly worn down. Between 10 July and 31 October 1940 the RAF had lost around 788 aircraft, while the *Luftwaffe* had lost 1,294; and air supremacy over the Channel had still not been achieved. In the third week of September the invasion was postponed, and then in October shelved. At the cost of over 500 pilots killed, Fighter Command had won the Battle of Britain, thereby ensuring that the war would go on [60].

STRATEGIES FOR SURVIVAL AND EXPANSION, 1940–41

Churchill Looks West

Though the Battle of Britain disposed of the immediate invasion threat (though night bombing – the Blitz* – continued into 1941), for Churchill and his War Cabinet the position over the winter of 1940–41 was fraught with peril. Hitler was master of much of Europe, while Britain, even with help from the Dominions (Australia, Canada, South Africa, New Zealand) and other parts of the empire, was very much alone. Britain had survived, but to carry on the war and eventually to go over to the offensive American help was vital. In the medium term Churchill hoped that the United States would be drawn into the war as an ally; in the immediate future American financial and other aid would be critical.

For President Franklin D. Roosevelt* and other Americans who saw the triumph of Hitler in 1940 as a looming threat to the Western Hemisphere, aiding the British war effort seemed a good idea once it was clear that Britain was willing and able to fight on alone. There was, however, still a strong isolationist lobby in Congress, which meant the president would have to proceed cautiously. Britain was able to buy US small arms during the summer of 1940, but Britain's dollar reserves were rapidly dwindling. The first alternative to cash payment proposed by the Roosevelt administration was a straight trade: the United States would hand over fifty old destroyers in exchange for base leases in eight British possessions in the Western Hemisphere stretching from Newfoundland to the Caribbean. After a certain amount of haggling over the wording, this 'destroyers-for-bases' deal was agreed to at the beginning of September 1940. There were, however, only so many geographical assets that the United States wanted and Britain could trade: by the end of 1940, with Roosevelt having won his bid for re-election in November, it was clear that with Britain almost bankrupt more sweeping measures were in order.

Direct US financial aid was made impossible by memories of Britain defaulting on its loans from World War I and isolationist suspicions. Instead, Roosevelt conceived the Lend-Lease* Bill, the idea being that the United States would pass over the arms and material Britain needed to fight on, with arrangements for return or repayment to be made later. This, Roosevelt explained in a press conference, was like a man who lends his neighbour a garden hose to put out a fire, the emergency taking precedence over the question of return or repayment. The administration was able to argue that only by supporting Britain would the United States be able to stay out of the war, thereby managing to nullify isolationist claims that the bill would lead America into war (something that Roosevelt had promised would not happen during the presidential election campaign in the autumn of 1940). After a tough Congressional battle the Lend-Lease Bill became law in March 1941; in effect, expanding US arms and other industries were now placed at Britain's disposal. By the end of the war Britain had received about $22 billion worth of American food, oil, arms, aircraft, and vehicles [67, 70].

Hitler Turns East

Meanwhile, as London and other cities suffered through the Blitz and Churchill looked westward for help, Hitler had turned his attention eastward. Deteriorating relations with the USSR over the future of southeastern Europe, combined with the Führer's long-term goal of 'living space' in the East and the destruction of the 'Jewish–Bolshevik conspiracy', made a new *Blitzkrieg* against Stalin's Russia appear increasingly attractive. Britain, even with American aid, was for the time being barred from the Continent and might be neutralized through the U-boat* campaign, while the Soviet Union was and would remain a major threat to Germany. As early as June 1940 Hitler had ordered planning for such an operation to begin, and by December plans for a full-scale invasion of western Russia in the summer of 1941, Operation Barbarossa,* were being put into place and forces shifted eastward. Before Barbarossa could take place, however, the southern flank would have to be secured [72].

The Mediterranean and the Balkans

One difficulty Hitler faced as he contemplated turning east was the mess his ally, Mussolini, had made since entering the war in June 1940. Hoping to get in on the spoils the *Duce** had sent Italian forces northward, only to see them repulsed by the French. The subsequent Italian contribution to the Battle of Britain also had been a disaster. At Mussolini's insistence, Italian forces in Libya had cautiously advanced into British-held Egypt in September 1940; only to be ejected and sent reeling back towards Tripoli by a few British infantry divisions and tank units in subsequent months. Doubtless hoping for an easier target, Mussolini launched an invasion of Greece from Albania (occupied since 1939) in October 1940, only to see the Greek army first halt and then roll back the Italian invasion force. In November 1940 the Royal Navy scored a singular success when torpedo planes put out of action half the Italian fleet at anchor in Taranto. In North Africa, reinforced British units under the overall command of General Archibald Wavell* had, by February 1941, advanced 1,700 miles westward, destroying ten Italian divisions at the cost of a mere 2,000 casualties [62].

From the perspective of Berlin, if something was not done soon, the Italians might well be ejected from Libya altogether. The British might also use Greece (which had as yet declared war only on Italy) as a base for air operations against the oil fields of Romania that were vital to the German war effort.

Something was done. German plans to invade Greece were formulated as early as October 1940, and in February 1941 the first air and ground units (the beginnings of the famous Afrika Korps*) arrived in Libya to prop up the Italians. The southern flank would have to be secured before the main German campaign of 1941 – Barbarossa – got under way. In April, German forces were allowed to pass through Romania and Bulgaria, and after a brief fight in Yugoslavia these forces invaded Greece. Australian and New Zealand units as well as some RAF aircraft were diverted from the Western Desert to try and shore up Greek resistance, but this action merely weakened Wavell's army just as Rommel began his first offensive in April–May 1941 and

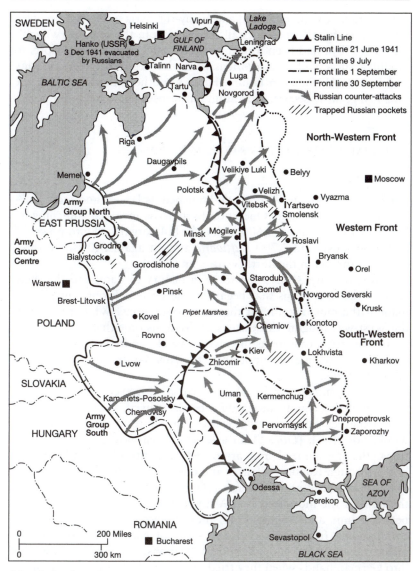

Map 2. Barbarossa
Source: *The Second World War*, John Keegan, Hutchinson, London, 1989,
p. 183.

did little to help the Greeks. By the end of April the last British forces
were being evacuated from Greece; forces that subsequently proved
unable, despite fierce resistance, to defeat a German airborne invasion
of Crete in May 1941. By this time, though the Italian Empire in East

Africa had fallen and both Iraq and Vichy-run Syria were soon occupied (in a successful effort to forstall Axis moves in the region), Wavell's forces in Libya had been forced to retreat back into Egypt. Efforts to mount a successful counteroffensive in the Western Desert in May and June 1941 ended in failure. Hitler's southern flank was, for the time being, fairly secure. Operation Barbarossa could begin [66, 68].

THE LIMITS OF *BLITZKRIEG*, 1941–42

Barbarossa

On 22 June 1941 the *Wehrmacht* launched its largest and most ambitious campaign to date. Operation Barbarossa involved launching no less than 146 divisions, 3,600 tanks (the bulk organized into powerful Panzer groups), and 2,700 *Luftwaffe* aircraft against Russia in three powerful thrusts in the north, centre, and south.

It was the largest invasion force in history to date, and the sheer scale of the operations that began on the Eastern Front immediately made it the most significant theatre of operations. While the war in the West was fought with dozens of divisions on either side, the war in the East from first to last involved several hundred divisions at any one time. In scale and importance, the Russo–German war dwarfed all other fronts.

In the opening months of Barbarossa, however, it looked very much as if this significance would be short-lived. Complete surprise was achieved, Stalin having willed himself to believe that Hitler would not attack [*Doc. 6*]. In a series of fast-moving pincer operations, the mechanized and armoured elements of the *Wehrmacht* broke through Russian defences and created a series of pockets in the Bialystock–Minsk and Smolensk regions, and later at Kiev, in which the bulk of the mobilized Red Army was surrounded and destroyed between June and August 1941. Inexperienced Soviet commanders, commanding formations critically short of communications equipment, transport and enough modern weapons, time and again played into German hands when they tried to obey Stalin's orders to counter-attack rather than retreat.

Soviet losses were staggering. In the Bialystock and Minsk pockets alone over half a million Red Army soldiers were captured or killed, and 2,500 tanks and 1,500 guns lost. Between July and September, a grand total of fourteen Soviet armies were surrounded and destroyed, Red Army losses had mounted into the millions, and the vast bulk of the 15,000 tanks and 8,000 aircraft located in western Russia and

Poland in June 1940 had ceased to exist. By late August the *Wehrmacht* had advanced hundreds of miles eastward and had reached the Dnieper river. To many observers it seemed as if it was only a matter of time before the Soviet Union collapsed [73].

Despite the huge losses in the summer and autumn of 1941, however, the Red Army survived. This was largely due to its sheer potential size, which German planners had underestimated by about 50 per cent, and the ability of the Soviet authorities to relocate key war industries to points in the Urals and Transcaucasus beyond German reach. With huge manpower reserves to draw upon, by December 1941 the Red Army had created and deployed almost 200 new divisions. Thus, even after the equivalent of 100 divisions had been lost, the Red Army (though short of equipment and training) could keep on fighting. Moreover, the German victories had not been achieved without cost. By the beginning of August the Germans had lost 179,500 men in battle, while tank strength was being steadily whittled down through battlefield attrition and wear and tear. By September, for example, the 3rd Panzer Group had lost 59 per cent of the tanks with which it had begun the campaign. Given the state of German industry, these were losses hard to replace.

Yet in the wake of the stunning success of the Kiev encirclement battle, Hitler and his commanders still believed that Moscow could be taken before the end of the year by concentrating Panzer forces for one last thrust. Initially, the drive on Moscow went well, with yet more pockets being created at Briansk and Vyazma in October 1941 in which over 660,000 prisoners, 1,242 tanks, and 5,412 artillery pieces were taken and eight armies destroyed.

By this time, however, the *Wehrmacht* was overextended and suffering significantly from the effects of four months of hard fighting against a foe who refused to admit that he was beaten. By October one-sixth of the men of the invasion force had been lost, and replacements had nowhere near matched losses. One last lunge at Moscow after the autumn rains in October–November failed to win the prize, the Soviets having concentrated fresh forces from the Far East around the capital. Barbarossa had failed [76].

The Soviet Winter Counteroffensive

The Red Army, moreover, directed by some of the more competent surviving commanders such as Semyon Timoshenko and Georgi Zhukov, had marshalled just enough strength to launch a counterattack in December 1941 at the very point when the *Wehrmacht* was at its weakest. The initial Red Army thrusts around Moscow and elsewhere caused consternation among German commanders and generated calls for a general withdrawal. Hitler would have none of it. He relieved large numbers of generals, took personal command of the army, and issued orders to stand fast. Luckily for the *Wehrmacht*, with many of its now very weak divisions dangerously exposed or cut off, Stalin became overly confident and in January ordered a general counteroffensive. This dissipated the still limited strength of the Red Army, and large-scale encirclements attempted were often beyond the capacity of new formations and their commanders. Though some local successes were achieved and the Germans driven back from Moscow, the Soviet counteroffensive failed to achieve any decisive breakthroughs. The future of the Russo–German war still hung in the balance. *Blitzkrieg* had degenerated into attritional slogging, the *Wehrmacht* had been stopped, but not defeated. Only in the wake of summer and autumn campaigns of 1942 would it become clear which side had what it took to win [74].

America goes to War

In the course of 1941 American aid to Britain had steadily increased: and not only in terms of Lend–Lease. From April onward US warships and aircraft operating in the Western Atlantic served a reconnaissance function in the British war against the U-boats. In July the British garrison of Iceland began to be replaced by American troops. In August Roosevelt, Churchill, and their chief military advisors had met for the first time aboard ships anchored off the Newfoundland coast, and issued a statement indicating common commitment to the preservation of democracy. By September increasing friction over the US supporting role in the Western Atlantic had produced an attack on a US warship and in response a presidential order that U-boats be sunk on sight in areas patrolled by American warships. Other 'incidents' followed, and US–German relations deteriorated further.

Congress, however, remained cautious, and it is unlikely that full-scale American intervention would have taken place if Hitler, in the wake of the Japanese attack on Pearl Harbor, had not declared war on the United States on 10 December. Professions of Axis solidarity with Japan aside, it seems likely that the Führer saw war looming with America in the near future and wanted to appear strong by taking the initiative on the matter. 'I'll never believe that an American soldier can fight like a hero,' was his dismissive comment (17 *p. 149*).

In the short term America's entry into the war at the side of Britain and Russia had only a limited effect. The armed forces, the US army in particular, were only just beginning to expand, and the needs of the

British and Russians for tanks and aeroplanes, along with the competing priorities of the war against Japan, meant that it would be several
months before American ground and air forces could be equipped and
deployed to the European theatre in any numbers. However, along
with having to face a long war with the Soviet Union, it was Hitler's
decision to range the United States among his enemies, along with the
looming prospect of a long war in Russia, that transformed a war of
Blitzkrieg conquests into a drawn-out total war that Germany was ill-
equipped to win.

3   PEOPLES AT WAR

ECONOMIES AND SOCIETIES AT WAR

Germany

If judged by the success of its military campaigns in the first years of the war, the productive capacity of the Third Reich was quite adequate. With only limited centralized direction of labour and resources by the state, the slowly expanding output of steel, coal, synthetic oil, and other industrial essentials was sufficient to sustain – but not significantly augment – the material needs of the armed forces. German aircraft production, for example, was only 13 per cent greater in 1941 than it had been in 1940, while production of automatic weapons actually fell over the same period.

The weapons and equipment produced, moreover, tended to be modifications of existing models rather than new types. The tanks and aircraft with which Germany fought the war through 1940–42 were essentially upgraded versions of the most advanced types in service in 1939: the Bf-109 fighter, for example, or the marks III and IV Panzer (tank).

In essence this meant that in the years of *Blitzkrieg* the German war economy was not significantly different from that of peacetime (bearing in mind that the peacetime economy had itself been heavily aligned towards expansion of the armed forces). If victory could be secured on these terms, this was acceptable; and indeed desirable, given Hitler's great reluctance to impose heavy burdens on the civilian populace. This, in his view, was what had caused Germany to collapse in 1918, so direction of civilian labour and rationing were avoided as much as possible.

By 1942, however, it was clear that the years of easy victories were past. Germany now faced a coalition of Great Powers, two of which at least possessed very powerful economies indeed. Hence, after Albert Speer* was appointed minister for war production in February 1942, efforts to rationalize and streamline the war economy accelerated dramatically. Competition for resources between services and industries was reduced, production tailored to available resources and labour, and priority given to development of a few new weapons (such as the Tiger and Panther tanks designed to outmatch Soviet armour) and mass production of a limited number of existing items (such as the Bf-109 fighter). Older men, as well as women, were partially mobilized for war work in 1943, and in 1944 full wage and price controls as well as more stringent and extensive rationing scales were introduced. The civilian economy, in short, became more and more a true war economy [25].

War production increased dramatically. In 1942, for example, German factories had turned out 9,300 tanks, only a few thousand more than in 1941 (5,200) and 1940 (2,200). In 1943, however, the annual total jumped to 19,800, and to a peak of 27,300 in 1944. A similar situation existed with military aircraft and their engines, with annual production peaking in 1944 at between three and four times the 1940 figure.

Longer hours and more streamlined production only partly explain this increase. The constant demands of the *Wehrmacht*, combined with a political desire not to move too many women from civilian employment or the home into war factories, meant that the pool of available German workers was restricted. Luckily for Speer, however, the Third Reich could also draw on the vast foreign labour reserves created by conquest. By 1944 over 7 million foreigners were being employed in the greater Reich, both voluntary and (more often) conscripted skilled and semi-skilled labour being imported from Western Europe while the bulk of unskilled manual labour was forcibly brought in from the East in the form of prisoners of war and uprooted civilians from the Soviet Union. Among other things this allowed for more German labour to be shifted into war production from agriculture and the civilian economy than would otherwise have been the case, as well as providing a vast pool of slave workers for heavy manual work. The occupied territories also contributed to the war economy in the form of food requisitions.

Despite the scale of German conquest and the impressive rationalization and increases in output the German economy experienced in the 'total war' phase of the conflict, the Third Reich faced problems in key areas that could only be partially overcome. There was, to begin with, the fact that the population base (around 76 million in 1939), was much smaller than that of its combined adversaries, with concomitant effects on available military manpower and the civilian workforce that foreign labour could only ameliorate – especially as, for ideological reasons, the mobilization of women for factory work was more limited than in other countries [89].

As for POWs and slave labourers, they had little positive incentive to work hard. In the case of those from the East the quantity and quality of food and shelter provided was so poor that their capacity to work was far below potential in any event.

Hitler's personal interventions in the war production process in the later part of the war also sometimes flew in the face of the best utilization of resources. There was, for example, his insistence on trying to convert the Messerschmitt 262 – the world's first jet fighter and an aircraft that might have turned the air war in Germany's favour – into a fighter-bomber, which delayed its introduction into front-line service by at least a year. On a grander scale, Hitler's constant desire to strike back rather than defend what he still held funnelled resources into the rocket programme, the end result being the V-1s and V-2s* that enabled Germany once more to bombard London in 1944 but did nothing to alter the dramatically declining fortunes of the German armed forces in the West.

More significant in overall terms was the fact that Germany simply lacked key natural resources such as rubber, high-grade iron ore and oil. Nazi conquests, and being senior ally of such countries as oil-rich Romania, along with an effort to devise and manufacture substitutes, could only partially fill the gap between the needs of war – in practice the ability to match the enemy's output – and the available raw materials [95].

The effects of the disparity in human and material resources were clear to even the most optimistic Germans by the later stages of the war as enemy forces closed in on the Reich and Allied aircraft increasingly dominated the skies. In contrast to the last phase of the First World War, however, Germany society did not seriously fracture under the strains of looming defeat.

Though small resistance groups did exist in German society, no mass uprisings or mutinies ever occurred. Those few senior officers within the army who actively sought to depose Hitler recognized that success would depend on a *coup d'état* rather than popular discontent: hence the various bomb plots – none of which came off successfully – to kill Hitler and install a military government [120].

Passive loyalty to the regime was due in part to the degree of control exercised at home by the Nazi Party and the security organs of the state (such as the Gestapo*), while at the front, draconian punishments provided an incentive for ordinary soldiers to fight on even under the most adverse conditions (over 15,000 German soldiers, for example, were shot for not carrying out orders to the letter).

At least as important as coercion, however, was the way in which ordinary Germans in and out of uniform were persuaded that Germany was waging a war of racial survival and thus actively supported the Reich. The Ministry of Propaganda under Josef Goebbels* successfully played up the Nazi worldview in the press and cinema, while the young were indoctrinated by organizations such as the Hitler Youth and soldiers at the front by political education officers within the *Wehrmacht* itself as well as the increasingly large and more ideologically driven *Waffen-* [armed] *SS.** The appalling conditions of life and combat on the Eastern Front helped crystallize an image of war-to-the-death, while the bombing of German cities and the declared Allied policy of unconditional surrender gave credence to Goebbels' calls for greater sacrifices in order to avoid annihilation by Germany's enemies [*Doc. 11*]. Germans, in short, soldiered on to the bitter end [87, 106].

Italy

The same could not be said of Italians, for the simple reason that the war effort Mussolini initiated in 1940 was both unsuccessful in the field and poorly run at home. Lack of natural resources, especially fuels and other imported raw materials, imposed severe limits on war production. Despite a population nearly the size of Britain's, Italy in 1942, for example, managed to turn out a mere 2,400 aircraft; the same number as in 1941. Italian arms production was limited further by the inability of the Fascist state, rife with corruption, to rationalize production and engage in development. Thus, in order to protect the Fiat–Adalsano oligopoly, even the relatively small number of tanks produced remained seriously inferior even to British tanks. Meanwhile, the inability to consolidate the efforts of rival firms meant that even the best Italian combat aircraft, if produced by a small firm such as Macchi, had to compete for resources with larger companies such as Fiat that were producing greater quantities of inferior aircraft.

Efforts to pay for the war by printing more paper lire – the amount in circulation quadrupled between 1940 and 1943 – did little to curb the mounting deficit (64.5 billion lire in 1940–41, 84.8 billion lire in 1941–42) and of course set off massive inflation and a wage and price spiral. On the free market the value of the lire had declined seven times over in the course of the war. State efforts at rationing were both too harsh and, at the same time, ineffective due to an inability to control the black market.

Added to all this was humiliation on the battlefield, where success was only scored under the direction of German generals whose men regarded their allies with ill-concealed contempt. Little wonder, therefore, that by the spring of 1943, with the Allies poised to invade, strikes and other forms of protest were matched by the desire of the old elites (notably within the army) to ditch Mussolini and take Italy out of the war [128].

The Soviet Union

The survival of the USSR in 1941–42 was a true test of the strength of the Soviet command economy and state apparatus. Despite the destruction of most of its mobilized army, the loss of half its coal fields and steel production facilities to the Germans, and serious reversals at the front that continued into 1942, the strength and power of the Soviet armed forces steadily grew. Over 2,500 critical production facilities were relocated beyond the Urals and the Volga and points further east, and Herculean efforts were made to streamline and rationalize production of key weapons such as the T-34* medium tank (the best of the war) and Il-2* ground-attack aircraft. Despite ongoing shortages and crises, the directed Soviet war economy, drawing on a still quite enormous resource base, was able to keep the army and air force going in 1941–42 and begin to supply them with the equipment they would need to drive the invaders back.

Allied aid in the form of Lend-Lease helped in areas where Soviet production was weakest (e.g. trucks), but it was the Soviet economy itself that bore the brunt of war production demands. Even in 1941, as much of European Russia was being overrun, production of rugged tanks and aircraft was greater than in Germany (though losses were higher); by 1942 Soviet tank and aircraft production was significantly outstripping that of the Third Reich. In 1943–44, despite greatly increased German production, the USSR turned out almost 6,000 more tanks and self-propelled guns and over 10,000 more combat aircraft (see Tables 2–3).

The cost to the civilian economy was high. Much prime agricultural land as well as millions of workers had been lost to the Germans. Even with longer hours enforced on those collective farms still under the control of the Soviets, this loss – combined with lack of investment in agricultural machinery – meant that food production as well as the availability of consumer goods plummeted. Human and natural resources were ruthlessly exploited by the state to meet the needs of war. All labour was directed which, among other things, meant a greater proportion of women in industry and the armed

Table 2   *Wartime Aircraft Production Figures*

State	1939	1940	1941	1942	1943	1944	1945
USA	5,856	12,804	26,277	47,836	85,898	96,318	49,761
USSR	10,382	10,565	15,735	25,436	34,900	40,300	20,900
UK*	8,190	16,149	22,694	28,247	30,963	31,036	14,145
Germany	8,295	10,247	11,776	15,409	24,807	39,807	7,540
Italy	1,800	1,800	2,400	2,400	1,600	—	—
Japan	4,467	4,768	5,088	8,861	16,693	28,180	11,066

* Includes the Commonwealth.

Table 3   *Tank Production Figures, 1940–1944*

State	1940	1941	1942	1943	1944
Germany	2,200	4,800	9,300	19,800	27,300
USSR	2,700	6,500	24,400	24,000	28,900
USA	400	4,200	23,800	29,400	17,500
UK	1,400	4,800	8,600	7,400	5,000

forces (including – uniquely – the combat arms) as manpower dwindled. Hours were long, working conditions harsh, and rations and other incentives for even the most favoured skilled workers in war industries, meagre.

The security apparatus of the state, even more pervasive than in Germany, was partly responsible for maintaining public commitment to Stalin's regime. The appalling way in which the Nazis ruled the occupied territories of Russia and the Ukraine and treated Soviet prisoners left Soviet citizens with little choice but to support the regime. Public support for the war effort, however, was largely based on a successful appeal to patriotic instincts. The state propaganda apparatus, including commissars within the Red Army, portrayed the war in terms of national liberation rather than the class struggle. Fighting for Mother Russia proved far more appealing than fighting for an abstraction such as socialism, as even Stalin recognized. The peoples of the Soviet Union (numbering over 170 million) endured more hardship than anyone else and, drawing on their natural resources, outproduced and ultimately ground down their adversary [80].

Great Britain

Despite being able to draw upon the resources of the British Empire and the Commonwealth, the United Kingdom reached the limit of its war potential relatively early on in the war. As already noted, survival necessitated increasing reliance on financial and other aid from the United States in 1940–41. The war economy thus depended to a great extent on external support. Moreover, though supplemented by the efforts of the Dominions, the relatively small size of the British population (47 million) exposed limits to the size of both the war economy and the armed forces by 1943–44. Civilian consumption was regulated through rationing, and virtually all labour progressively mobilized, women included (though as elsewhere in the West traditional assumptions concerning gender roles set limits to female participation [98]).

However, only so much could be done. In 1944, for example, with the British army at its maximum strength of over 2,700,000, British industry produced only 5,000 tanks, and through much concentration of effort slightly increased aircraft production to reach the maximum annual figure of 26,461 [84].

Moreover, due to structural weaknesses in British industry as well as poor design, certain essential war items were more costly to produce and less combat worthy than their German equivalents. British combat aircraft by the late stages of the war were, for example, second to none yet relatively costly to produce; while British trucks and tanks were inferior in almost every respect [81].

Still, the British effort was in many respects an impressive one, especially for a cash-strapped democracy trying to fight a total war. Rationing and the allocation of labour were both handled with fairness and skill, and blatant propaganda usually eschewed in favour of (selectively) telling the truth. Though legal sanctions existed and were sometimes used, the success of the British war effort ultimately depended on the willingness of the British people to make voluntary sacrifices. Despite strikes and lack of commitment in some sections of the population [*Doc. 13*], the war effort from 1940 onward did generate a very real sense of unity within Britain. Though well-meant efforts to strengthen morale in the armed forces and civilian sectors produced little response, it is worth remembering that the authorities never thought British conscripts and volunteers needed the kind of draconian coercive measures common in both the German and Soviet armies to prevent collapse [*Doc. 22*]. All wartime myths aside, there really did exist a consensus that Hitler should be defeated and that sacrifices would have to be made.

The United States

The American war economy was by far the most successful of all the belligerents. This was largely because of the latent prewar strength of the United States in workers, raw materials, modern industries, and mass production techniques [*Doc. 14*]. Because of the lingering effects of the Great Depression, there was still widespread unemployment and much underutilized plant before the war. But when the Roosevelt administration, working through the War Production Board and other new agencies, began to pour huge amounts into the war effort through deficit financing ($57 billion worth by 1943), the latent potential of modern American industry to expand, adapt, and produce the sinews of war in astronomical quantities was actualized.

Huge new assembly-line factories, employing tens of thousands of workers, were quickly built for everything from heavy bombers to synthetic rubber. Unemployment disappeared as industry boomed and the armed forces expanded through the draft and volunteers (over 8 million in the army and air force alone by 1945).

Mass production techniques reached new heights in shipbuilding, where prefabrication of parts meant that 'Liberty' merchant ships* could be assembled like model kits. The output was phenomenal across the board. In 1943, when production had not yet reached its peak, US firms produced over 29,000 tanks and over 86,000 combat aircraft, not to mention vast quantities of everything else needed to fight a modern war. Much of it, furthermore, was well designed and of high quality. There was enough to equip not only the American armed forces fighting a two-front war but also, through Lend-Lease, to give substantial help to the Allies. By the end of the war the United States had produced 40 per cent of all the weapons produced by all the belligerents combined [99].

Moreover, though civilian production was curtailed, rationing of fuel became necessary, and working hours were lengthened, the demand for labour in a free market meant that the wages and standard of living of war industry workers went up. The demand for labour was also great enough to bring approximately 4 million women into the workforce as munitions workers, riveters, welders, and more traditional office workers (though traditional assumptions concerning gender roles had an effect on both pay scales and popular expectations of a return to hearth and home for women after the war [79]). Inflation, meanwhile, was curbed through a successful government campaign to get people to invest in war bonds and other savings rather than spend, while the huge national debt was made bearable by keeping interest rates artificially low.

Overall, the sacrifices required of Americans were far lower than in other belligerent countries even as American factories outproduced friend and foe alike. Even in the US armed forces pay and conditions were significantly better than in the services of other countries. Morale was generally high, sustained by government 'information' agencies and a vast Hollywood public relations machine that softened the realities of actual combat. When American forces first went into action the tenacity and skill of their adversaries came as a shock; but with the world's greatest war machine behind them the armed forces adapted tactics and weaponry to suit the occasion and self-confidence returned.

BARBARISM AND THE HOLOCAUST

Barbarism

Industrial might and technological sophistication played major roles in determining both the course and the costs of the Second World War. So, too, did the ideological dimension of the conflict, making it among the most barbaric wars of modern times.

In the West the ideological dimension of the war and its effect on behaviour was limited. Though state propaganda on the Allied side presented the struggle as one fought to safeguard democracy against tyranny, and on the Axis side as a war fought to achieve supremacy, in the face of malignant foreign powers and international capitalism, enemy personnel were still regarded as part of a more-or-less common humanity. POWs, therefore, and enemy civilians in occupied areas, were treated with at least a modicum of respect and adherence to international law, at least in the early years.

As the war went on, to be sure, the commitment in the West to fighting a 'clean' war (that is, according to international agreements such as the 1929 Geneva Convention* regarding POWs) came under serious strain. Military necessity tended to erode civilian noncombatant status on both sides. The need to strike at war industries and the enemy will to wage war came to justify the bombing of cities after only a relatively brief period of restraint. Restrictions on the sinking of civilian and neutral shipping were ditched just as fast in order to make submarines effective in waging economic warfare.

By the middle of the war ideological considerations mixed with presumed military necessity were making the war between German occupation forces and resistance groups in Western Europe very brutal. In countries where a formal armistice had been signed such as France, armed resistance fighters were viewed and treated as renegades without the rights of formal combatants and thus liable to be sent to a concentration camp or shot out of hand if caught. By its very nature guerilla warfare meant holding prisoners in accordance with the Geneva Convention was impossible for resistance movements. Thus little mercy was shown towards captives taken by either side.

Increasingly, moreover, the German military and security authorities resorted to indiscriminate hostage-taking and mass reprisals to retaliate and undermine public support for the Resistance. By the spring and summer of 1944 increased resistance activity in France was met in several instances by the systematic destruction of entire villages and the murder of everyone found in them.

Even formal combatants, who normally enjoyed the privileges of POW status in the West, could become victims of retaliation and prejudice. Hitler issued secret orders that British commandos, who did not 'fight fair', should be executed when captured. Both sides murdered small numbers of more conventional war prisoners at and behind the front, particularly during periods of heavy bombing and brutal combat in which the desire for revenge became inflamed. The more ideologically committed and ruthless elements within the German armed forces were also capable of murdering POWs in larger numbers; the *Waffen-SS* – the fighting branch of the Nazi security force (the SS) which Hitler allowed to be built into multiple-division strength as the war progressed – being particularly prone to shoot down groups of surrendered enemy personnel in cold blood.

It was in the East, however, that ideological considerations much more profoundly influenced behaviour in a negative manner. In the East, racial and political ideology precipitated a descent into barbarism of a scale unknown in the West.

In Hitler's view, the Slavic people of the East were a significantly inferior race occupying living space that would better be utilized by superior Aryan (i.e. unsullied German) stock. In the Soviet Union, moreover, a regime existed based on a political philosophy that was the very antithesis of National Socialism: Communism. This was a view held widely, if not always quite so virulently, in much of German society, and it had a considerable impact on how conquered peoples were handled right from the start.

Lack of initial armed resistance and a high level of industrial development in portions of the country (industries that could best be exploited by the local work force) meant that the Czechs, under German rule in the Reich protectorates of Bohemia and Moravia since March 1939, were treated with comparative leniency. Only selected villages and towns were razed, and 'only' 350,000 inhabitants were executed or otherwise died as a result of the Nazi occupation.

Plans existed for the deportation and elimination of the Czechs once the war was over; such plans for the Poles were put straight into effect in the wake of Poland's fighting stand in September 1939. Even as the *Wehrmacht* advanced, SS special parties following behind engaged in a systematic effort to find and kill known Polish patriots as well as other undesirable elements. Warsaw was the first city to experience concentrated aerial bombardment at a time when cities were deliberately avoided as targets in the West. During the fighting, and subsequently, the German armed forces and security services destroyed dozens of towns and villages and shot thousands of civilians who had the misfortune to belong to an 'inferior' race. The western portion of Poland was incorporated directly into the Reich, and, in order to make way for ethnic German settlers, the million Polish inhabitants were simply evicted and dumped under brutal conditions further east in the winter of 1939–40. The remainder of German-occupied Poland, the so-called General Government, was systematically plundered for food and other resources without regard for the survival of the Poles who lived or were dumped there. Under the rule of Hans Frank* and other Nazi figures, the native population was rapidly reduced to the status of sub-human slaves whose native culture had to be eradicated and whose purpose would have been served after most of them had died off in the harshly governed labour camps established to maximize their immediate benefit to the Third Reich. Even without the Jewish population being taken into account, several million Poles died as a result of all this.

What had been started in Poland was continued, on a grander scale, after the western portions of the Soviet Union were overrun in the second half of 1941. Special orders were issued to the *Wehrmacht* making it clear that the new foe was to be regarded with extreme ruthlessness. Once the invasion had begun, special SS groups made sure that the order to kill all captured commissars was carried out. The *Wehrmacht*, meanwhile, already primed to view the war in the East as one in which moral scruples had no place, was confirmed in its attitude of extreme brutality toward civilian and soldier alike by the viciousness of the fighting and the way in which partisan activity sprang up behind the lines. By the winter 1941–42, if not before, the armed forces were treating every Russian encountered as a sub-human threat to be exploited or eliminated [107].

In the conquered Eastern Territories the Nazi policy was similar to that pursued in Poland. Despite some initial enthusiasm in regions such as the Ukraine for liberation from communism, the resident Slav populations were uniformly regarded and treated as sub-human by their new rulers. Mass executions, deportations of hundreds of thousands of inhabitants, confiscation and destruction of property, and plundering of food and other resources were systematically undertaken. The millions of Ukrainian and other Soviet civilians forcibly sent to work in the Reich were generally treated with far more brutality and callousness than their counterparts from Western Europe. As many as ten million civilian citizens died as a result of Nazi occupation policies [*Doc. 10*] [117].

Soviets in uniform fared no better. Quite apart from the commissars, many individuals and small groups of captured Red Army troops were simply shot out of hand by *Wehrmacht* troops as vermin or in retaliation for fighting too hard or for the real or imagined murder and mutilation of German personnel. As for the huge numbers of men captured *en masse* in the great encirclement battles of 1941, what might be termed a policy of malevolent neglect and overwork meant that the majority died of starvation, exhaustion, and disease while confined in vast holding pens, in transit to Germany, or in permanent POW labour camps in the Reich. Soviet POWs were regarded and treated as animals, and up to three million – out of five million taken – died as a result.

The odds were also against survival for those German soldiers taken by the Soviets. The brutal nature of the Stalinist regime meant that the shooting of prisoners was actively encouraged by the state propaganda apparatus until labour needs made captured personnel more valuable in the second half of the war. Even then, the incredible brutality of German occupation policies made the enemy seem completely inhuman: and thus not worthy of mercy. When the Red Army broke into eastern Germany in 1945, soldiers were in effect encouraged to wreak a terrible revenge by looting, raping and killing civilians at random. As for the large groups of German POWs captured at Stalingrad in 1943 and elsewhere, those who were not killed outright were sent back to perform hard labour for the Soviet Union without adequate food, clothing, or shelter. Living and working conditions were such that a million or so died before the last of the surviving three million odd German POWs were repatriated in the early 1950s [114].

The war in the East, in short, was even more brutal than the war in the West. The ultimate in barbarism, however, was reserved for the Jewish population of Europe both East and West.

The Holocaust

Neither popular nor state-sponsored anti-Semitism were anything new in European history by the time the Nazis came to power in 1933. The (unfounded) belief that the Jews exercised undue control of financial and cultural affairs to the detriment of Gentiles was common in most parts of Europe in the first part of the twentieth century. It was only in Germany, however, that a regime existed in which solving the 'Jewish Problem' was a central concern.

In the Nazi scheme of things the root of all evil was the Jew. To Hitler and his followers the Jews collectively constituted an absolute evil, constantly seeking to undermine the Aryan race and thereby achieve world domination. Even in the midst of a world war the Jews remained the ultimate enemy in the eyes of Hitler and most of his followers. Indeed, the eventual solution to the 'Jewish Problem' suggests that, in ideological terms, the destruction of the European Jews was a necessary component of total war.

Nazi action against Jews, both in 1930s Germany and subsequently in the occupied parts of Western Europe, was initially confined to legal measures designed to disempower them and to occasional outbursts of state-inspired violence. Those labelled Jewish – anyone with a Jewish grandparent – were systematically barred from the professions, forced to wear the yellow star of David, and in general deprived of the rights of citizens. Before the war, and even to a limited extent in 1939–40, Jews were also encouraged to emigrate abroad.

The onset of war in the East, however, heralded the beginning of systematic brutality and violence. Thousands of Jews were among those Polish civilians wantonly killed in the war's opening campaign. In 1940–41 the remaining 2.5 million Polish Jews and many of the remaining German Jews were concentrated in overcrowded and unsanitary ghettos in urban centres such as Warsaw and Lodz where, on rations even more limited than those allowed to other Poles, thousands died of disease and starvation. It was only with the invasion of the Soviet Union in the summer of 1941, however, that systematic murder began to be practiced against Jews.

Special SS killing squads followed the armies eastward with orders to eliminate not only commissars and other communist functionaries but also all Jews. With the active help of anti-Semitic elements in the Baltic republics, Bessarabia, Moldavia and the Ukraine, Jews were rounded up and gunned down by the thousand. Over half a million men, women and children were shot or beaten to death by the killing squads and their local helpers within six months of the start of Barbarossa.

This, however, proved to be only the beginning of the slaughter. Up to this point the anti-Jewish measures taken were similar to those practiced in earlier times by other regimes (e.g. Imperial Russia). In late 1941 and early 1942, with emigration blocked off by the war and Germany now in control of the bulk of the European population, a unique and terrifyingly final solution* to the 'Jewish Problem' was adopted: genocide on an industrial scale.

Even as the first trials were being carried out with gas vans in the East (in which victims were killed by carbon monoxide poisoning), plans were drawn up in January 1942 for the systematic rounding up and deportation of all the European Jews to the East for 'resettlement': a euphemism for mass murder through the application of modern technology (such as the gas chamber) in a series of new SS death camps such as Treblinka whose sole purpose was to dispose of Jews as quickly as possible [*Doc. 25*]. Beginning in March 1942 the final solution was modified somewhat to accord with the needs of the war effort, so that at the huge Auschwitz–Birkenau concentration camp complex (the sixth of the death camps) the fitter adults were worked to death under appalling conditions in nearby industries while the remainder were gassed on arrival. Run with administrative thoroughness and technical ingenuity, the death camps in combination with the earlier killings and those that occurred after the last of the death camps was shut down in late 1944, claimed the lives of six million Jews (as well as hundreds of thousands of Gypsies, homosexuals, political prisoners, and other undesirables) [113].

What makes the Holocaust unique in the annals of human barbarity, even in the context of a total war in which millions more innocents were killed, was its goal and the machine-like thoroughness with which it was pursued. No other wartime campaign – for that is what it constituted – aimed at the physical destruction of an entire people. Millions of other Europeans died as a result of bombing, shooting, starvation, and other causes brought on directly or indirectly by enemy action. In all such cases, however, even the bloodiest, the primary aim was to break resistance rather than completely annihilate the enemy.

Who was responsible? In the narrowest sense the senior SS and other Nazi leaders who carried out the Führer's wishes and the ten thousand or so SS and other personnel directly involved in the death camps and shootings. On a wider scale it was the German security personnel and collaborationist authorities (including some German-sponsored Jewish councils) in Occupied Europe who registered, rounded up, and deported the Jews.

Though efforts were made to keep the final fate of deported Jews a secret, not least from the Jews themselves, news of the death camps did leak out; and those in authority who were seriously worried about the fate of the deportees managed, in some cases, to delay or entirely avert the final solution in some regions. Thus the majority of Danish Jews were secretly shipped to neutral Sweden, while the Finnish and Bulgarian governments – though German allies – stoutly refused to allow their Jews to be taken away. The same was true of Italy and Hungary until German forces actually occupied these countries and set up puppet regimes in September 1943 and March 1944 respectively. Elsewhere, however, most enthusiastically in the East but also in, for example, Vichy France, the local authorities collaborated in the rounding up and dispatch of Jews with more than an inkling of their ultimate fate.

COLLABORATION AND RESISTANCE

The fate of the Jews was only one of the areas in which the question of whether or how far to collaborate with, or resist the Germans, arose in Occupied Europe. Everywhere peoples and regimes produced an array of responses to German hegemony ranging from active collaboration to armed resistance. Though it was convenient after the war to assume that most Europeans were resisters of one sort or another and that collaboration was confined to marginal elements, the truth was rather more complex.

Collaboration

Co-operation with Germany, the primary occupying power on the Continent, took on a variety of forms and varied according to location and circumstance. At one end of the spectrum there was simple acceptance of the German presence, a live-and-let live philosophy. Beyond that there existed varying degrees of willingness to actively accommodate the Germans, in the hope that this would cause the least disruption to normal life and provide advantages in the postwar settlement. The attack on the Soviet Union helped draw in those who saw Bolshevism as the central threat to Europe. Many of these anti-communist collaborators – though by no means all – were members of various indigenous fascist groups eager to take their place in the Nazi New Order. They tended to occupy the far end of the collaborationist spectrum, and form the core of the military and paramilitary formations sponsored by the Germans to fight in the East or against the Resistance.

The number of extremist collaborators was relatively small. Though a few figures such as Vidkun Quisling* in Norway were placed in important administrative positions, indigenous fascist leaders such as Anton Mussert* (Holland) usually found the Germans more interested in a *modus vivendi* with the existing structures of authority than in promoting miniature Führers. Voluntary rank-and-file extremist collaborators usually numbered only in the thousands, and though sometimes effective in helping maintain order at home through para-military formations (the French *Milice*,* for example), their perform-ance as members of their own front-line unit or *Waffen-SS* units was variable at best and statistically insignificant. As for those who were drawn into extreme collaborationist ranks through compulsion, such as the tens of thousands of Soviet POWs who ended up in German uniform, their lack of commitment was reflected in their military per-formance, which ranged from mediocre to disastrous.

More limited collaboration was much more pervasive, especially in the West. Ministers in Vichy France were dedicated to restoring the nation through co-operation with the new masters of Europe. In the occupied zone of France (the entire country after November 1942) and elsewhere, German occupation forces established working rela-tionships with local victuallers and police, while individual Germans struck up personal relationships with local women. Businesses and industries, such as French truck plants, reoriented themselves to pro-vide for the German market. Vichy France and other semi-satellite regimes, meanwhile, sought with varying degrees of enthusiasm and commitment to accommodate themselves to the New Order while preserving and promoting their own interests. The bulk of Europe's population, through acceptance of the German presence, were, in effect, passive collaborators [121, 122].

Resistance

Not all, however, were willing to accept the German presence. There were those who fled either at the time of German invasion or later and created forces supported by the Allies such as the Free French of Charles de Gaulle* [*Doc. 5*]. There were also those left behind who from the first were prepared to resist. Their numbers grew as the more and more exploitative nature of the New Order in Europe made even passive collaboration seem less and less attractive. The British Special Operations Executive (SOE*), and later the American Office of Strategic Services (OSS*), provided organizational and logistical support on a limited scale when and where they thought appropriate, as did the Kremlin on an even more limited scale.

In the East the sheer barbarity of the occupation forces (be they German or satellite) from the first moment of contact made accommodation difficult to impossible, and thereby stimulated resistance. Especially in regions where road and rail communications were limited and when resistance forces were not deterred by reprisals directed against the civilian population, partisan activity could tie down significant numbers of enemy troops while disrupting enemy movements.

Partisan activity behind the Eastern Front, drawing on the tens of thousands of Red Army personnel cut off (but not caught) in the German encirclements of 1941, was of major significance. Better known, however, is the epic story of Tito's* Partisan army in Yugoslavia. Unlike the rival (non-communist) Chetnik* resistance movement under General Draza Mihailovic,* which eventually became collaborationist, Tito's men and women were not deterred from action against the Axis by even the most brutal of reprisals against Yugoslav civilians. Threatened by a series of Axis offensives and encirclement efforts and constantly on the move, Tito not only managed to survive but also strike back at the enemy. The British, realizing that the Chetniks were not going to fight the enemy, switched their logistical air-dropped support to Tito in 1943. By the following year there were over 250,000 fighting partisans, now operating offensively. Tito had become the *de facto* head of a new Yugoslav government, his troops storming into Belgrade alongside the Red Army in October 1944 [123].

Fighting resistance in the West took longer to develop. Military refugees fleeing Hitler's advance, including large numbers of Poles and later Frenchmen, were organized into units that evolved into brigades and divisions that eventually saw service in the Allied reconquest of Europe. But within Occupied Europe itself, the London authorities viewed intelligence work as the most useful immediate role that sympathizers could play, be it reporting on German troop movements or assisting the evasion efforts of downed Allied airmen. The formation of fighting resistance forces within France, Poland and elsewhere was supported by supplies and advisors from SOE and later the OSS; but these secret armies were, with the exception of those in the Balkans, supposed to remain in hiding and engage in only limited sabotage operations until the moment arrived for them to rise up in support of an Allied invasion [124].

Of perhaps even greater importance in limiting the profile of resistance in Western Europe was the relatively benign behaviour of German forces in the first years of the war. For communists the attack on the USSR was a key turning-point; for others it was the growing demands for labour to be sent to Germany in the latter part of the war, combined with the increasingly harsh and indiscriminate reprisals and other measures taken by the Gestapo and other security forces, which drove them off the fence and into the resistance camp. In southern France, for example, many young Frenchmen took to the hills and joined the *Maquis** (armed resistance bands) rather than be shipped off to Germany from the autumn of 1942 onwards.

The effectiveness of resistance forces supported by the Western Allies varied. Stronger motivation and higher comparative status made Free French and Polish divisions, for instance, as well as smaller contingents from other occupied countries, more effective as front-line forces than most collaborationist units. Much intelligence information and useful sabotage work was gained through the efforts of resistance groups in Occupied Europe. Where the opposing forces were weak or otherwise occupied, larger scale efforts to disrupt enemy communications and tie down local forces also met with success, as in June and August 1944 when the French forces of the interior (FFI*) assisted in the success of Allied landings on the coast. The unavoidable material weakness of such forces, however, especially in heavy weapons, meant that if regular German units could be brought to bear on them their chances of survival were slim. This was the fate of the *Maquis* who found themselves in the path of a *Waffen-SS* Panzer division hastening to Normandy in June 1944 and of the Polish Home Army* in Warsaw the following August, which, after initial success, was crushed by German forces unhindered by the nearby Red Army [119, 122].

4   CONDUCTING WAR

TECHNOLOGY AND INTELLIGENCE

The ability to produce war material in sufficient quantity was one factor in deciding how campaigns were conducted under conditions of total war. Just as important, however, was the capacity to improve weapons and – most important in the air and at sea – detection systems through the application of modern science. Also of vital importance was the ability to gain knowledge concerning the enemy's intentions while protecting one's own secrets. Spies, of course, were still used: but intelligence was also dependent to a considerable degree on a nation's level of technological skill as applied to signals coding and code-breaking.

Technology

On land, it must be said, while the technological quality of Italian arms continually lagged, the sophistication and quality of German industrial design and production meant that German equipment in the latter half of the war was limited in quantity but often of superior technological quality. Many German infantry weapons, especially machine guns and hand-held anti-tank weapons, were superior to their British, American, and Russian counterparts (as were the chemical and biological weapons that, fortunately, were never used). The newer German tanks were also very good. In response to the unexpected appearance of the heavily armed and well-armoured T-34 and KV-1 Russian tanks in 1941–42, German industry had not only successfully upgraded existing tanks such as the Mark III and Mark IV, but also developed and begun to deploy in 1943 the Mark V (Panther*) and Mark VI (Tiger*), both armed with high-velocity large calibre guns and very heavily armoured. Relatively sophisticated, these tanks were a match even for most Soviet mass-production tanks of the time such as the T-34/85, and seriously outclassed the much simpler and less well armed and armoured British and American medium tanks available in 1943–44 such as the Cromwell* and

Sherman.* (The sophistication and complexity of late-model German tanks – e.g. suspension systems – did, however, make them more costly and slower to produce.) [100]

A similar qualitative divergence existed with regard to anti-tank weapons – especially in relation to the famous German 88 mm anti-aircraft/anti-tank gun – and to some extent armoured personnel carriers. Only in medium and heavy artillery were the Russians, British and Americans at least the equal of the Germans in technological terms, and in the sinews of land warfare only in trucks were the Germans significantly inferior to the Americans in both quantity *and* quality; something which, paradoxically, made the *Wehrmacht* among the least mobile of major armies.

What this meant in practical terms was while Germany was slowly being borne down by weight of numbers, in individual engagements the technological superiority of German arms (combined with considerable tactical skill) could and did seriously impede the Allied march of conquest. On the Eastern Front, Soviet commanders considered a five-to-one superiority in men and equipment necessary if an attack were to succeed. In the West, during the Normandy fighting in 1944, the superiority of German armour was demonstrated time and again in tank battles: perhaps most graphically on 13 June when three Tigers ambushed a British column and knocked out 25 Cromwell tanks and other vehicles without loss [*Doc. 23*].

In the air, by contrast, it was the Allies who usually possessed a qualitative technological – as well as a very great numerical – advantage in the second half of the war. The development of truly modern Italian aircraft, as already noted, was hindered by political considerations. Development of new German aircraft types had been halted in 1940–41 when it seemed as if upgrading existing models would suffice; in the latter half of the war increased production, with only a few exceptions, took precedence over new designs (a number of which, especially among bombers, proved to be poorly thought out). The end result was that Soviet aircraft design was able to catch up to the Germans while the British and Americans drew ahead in the latter years of the war. The Soviet Yak-9* was the equal of the late-model Bf-109, for instance, while the American P-51 Mustang* was the best all-round piston-engined fighter of the entire war. German efforts to surge ahead in manned and unmanned aircraft design through the application of jet- and rocket-engine technology (the Messerschmitt 262* and 163* and the V-1* and V-2*) came to fruition too late and in too small a quantity in 1944–45 to seriously challenge Allied command of the air or cause serious damage on the ground.

The technological race to develop detection and counterdetection devices in the air war was more evenly matched, at least in the West where it counted most. To assist in night bombing, first Germany and then Britain and the United States developed radio beam and then radar navigation aids, while at the same time seeking ways to jam, confuse, or – in the case of navigation devices mounted in aircraft – home in on, enemy transmissions. To counter night bombing, both Britain and Germany not only improved ground radar systems for fighter direction and anti-aircraft gun laying, but also developed short-range airborne radar sets that could be mounted in twin-engined fighters, as well as homing and jamming devices. Among the most successful of these measures, used by the Allies to effect from 1943 onward, was WINDOW:* aluminium strips dropped in large quantities from aircraft which produced hundreds of false radar echoes [101].

The war at sea was also in part a struggle to deploy or counter more advanced detection devices and weaponry. Superiority swung back and forth, but at the time the war ended it was the Allies who held the upper hand technologically.

Mines were one focus of attention, especially in the first part of the war, with the Germans developing and deploying first magnetic and then acoustic mines and the British then developing countermeasures such as degaussing (which eliminated the magnetic field of a ship's hull) and sound magnification (which caused acoustic mines to explode prematurely). Late in the war the Germans deployed a new device off Normandy, the pressure mine (triggered by the changing water pressure over the mine caused by a ship's hull passing over-head), for which there was no obvious countermeasure: but by this time (1944) Allied material superiority was so great that the ship losses caused by the pressure mine could easily be made good.

Coming up with a means of defeating U-boat attacks on escorted merchant convoys occupied even more Allied attention, especially in the middle years of the war. This involved, among other things, developing more effective sonar* sets for warships to pin-point the location of submerged U-boats, high-frequency radar sets to detect the location of submarines on the surface that could be mounted both on escort vessels and (in addition to searchlights) on very long-range aircraft, and finally a new magnetic anomaly detection system. It also involved new weapon systems such as the British Hedgehog* and Squid*, designed to throw depth-charge bombs ahead of a ship (and so avoid losing sonar contact with an evading U-boat as the ship passed over-head in preparation for dropping conventional depth-charges).

The Italians failed to develop successful countermeasures to increase the effectiveness of their submarines. The Germans, on the other hand, developed counter-measures in the latter part of the war that included a snorkel device which allowed U-boats to run their diesel engines while remaining submerged, and radar warning devices. The Type VIIC and other U-boats of prewar design, however, remained too slow and limited in underwater range. By the time new engine and other technologies had been incorporated into the plans for a new generation of U-boats, such as the Type XXIII, the war was all but over.

In overall terms the Allies showed themselves able to develop and adapt, technologically, faster than the Germans in many (though by no means all) areas. Fast enough, at least, to bring the war to a close before a new generation of German aircraft and submarines could alter the balance of power in any serious way in the air or at sea.

Even on land, while still lagging behind the best German designs, British and American weapons became better as the war progressed. At the root this Allied advantage was because of the greater size of the scientific and material resources they could together deploy for research and development, as well as greater effort at co-ordination (plus the minds of refugee scientists) in research. It is significant that the R&D effort surrounding the most scientifically adventurous and technologically sophisticated weapon of all, the atomic bomb, was far more advanced in America (with aid from Britain and Canada) than it was in Germany when the war in Europe ended.

Intelligence and Deception

Knowledge about enemy movement, strength, and intentions could be obtained in several ways in World War II: through ground or aerial reconnaissance, through information obtained from captured personnel and equipment, through spies, or – and most importantly – through intercepting and decoding enemy signals. Conversely, efforts to deceive the enemy involved everything from camouflage to double-agents and false signals.

Aerial observation has advantages over the view from the front at ground level (where those advancing tend to get a better picture than those in retreat), and all air forces devoted some of their resources to reconnaissance over the battlefield and beyond. The success of this method of intelligence gathering depended to a great degree on the extent of air superiority already obtained. Though the British in particular modified a few of their best fighters for photographic reconnaissance purposes at the strategic level, on the tactical and operational level spotter planes were necessarily slow and thus vulnerable to attack. In effect this meant the side with command of the air (the Germans in France 1940 and Russia 1941–42, for instance, or the British and Americans over Normandy in 1944) got the best aerial intelligence.

The value of prisoners of war as a source of intelligence was limited, since few men of really senior rank were captured and the knowledge possessed by captured soldiers as to dispositions quickly became outdated. Captured equipment could yield up information as to strengths and weaknesses; but in most cases what was captured had already been rendered inoperable and thus of limited value. On occasion, however, special operations (such as the raid by British commandos in 1942 to seize a German radar set located on the enemy coast) or blind luck (as when a German night fighter equipped with a new type of radar landed in England by mistake in 1944) offered up enemy secrets.

As always, spies played a role in intelligence-gathering. Here the Germans were at a definite disadvantage, since the millions of foreign workers needed to keep the German war economy going might be used as intelligence sources by British intelligence organizations such as MI6* (the Secret Intelligence Service) and SOE,* and later by the American OSS. The same held true for the populations of the occupied territories, who could also shelter agents. Germany also suffered from an unusually high degree of competition and lack of co-ordination between rival intelligence agencies (the SD,* run by the SS, and the Abwehr,* run by the armed forces) as well as bad luck. Between them the spy services of the Soviet Union, the NKVD* (state security) and the GRU* (army intelligence), probably had the best human intelligence of all, having nurtured extensive spy rings all over Europe long before war broke out [102].

Of far greater overall importance to the course of the war than any of these sources of information, however, was signals intelligence. Intercepting enemy radio transmissions was a relatively simple matter; being able to decipher them was much more problematic. Careless use of ciphering equipment by diplomatic or military personnel, combined with a good deal of luck and guesswork, allowed both sides to eavesdrop on certain types of messages before systems were routinely modified or changed. In 1941, for instance, the British were able partially to anticipate U-boat moves after having broken the relevant code used in ship-shore transmissions, while in 1942 the Germans gained much useful information on convoy routes when they broke an important Allied naval cipher. Overall, however, especially in the second half of the war, it was the Allies who had the advantage in signals intelligence.

The British ability to read radio messages in a supposedly unbreakable cipher sent by all three German services using the Enigma* encrypting machine provided this advantage. The success of the British code breakers based at Bletchly Park in providing information from this source, codename 'Ultra',* was partly based on information concerning the Enigma machine provided by the Poles in 1939 and thereafter on the work of a group of brilliant mathematicians assisted, in 1944–45, by the first digital computer [103].

Since the Germans continued to believe the Enigma machine was foolproof (the Allies taking care to screen their source of information) while its users made careless mistakes in security procedure of which Bletchly Park could take advantage throughout the war, high-quality intelligence on German intentions was often available to British planners. The need to keep the source of Ultra intelligence a complete secret (so that the Germans would continue to use Enigma), combined with slow and patchy translation and guesswork in interpretation, meant that it was of limited use on a day-to-day basis in the first years of the war. Ultra was, however, of great significance in predicting both general trends throughout and more specific information as time passed. It was, for example, useful in assessing the strength and intentions of German forces in North Africa in 1942 and Normandy in 1944, in gauging the intentions of the Italian fleet in 1941, and from that year onward in allowing convoys to be diverted from the known path of U-boats: so much so that when the German naval cipher was made more complicated in 1942, causing a temporary blackout in Ultra information for several months, the loss of signals intelligence had a serious impact on convoy loss rates.

Though Ultra gave the Allies a singular advantage in signals intelligence, and at certain points was of great significance, it did not mean that British and American planners could always anticipate German moves. The true meaning of messages could be misinterpreted or ignored at Bletchly Park or by the senior commanders privy to the Ultra secret; so that, for example, information concerning enemy preparations for the 1941 invasion of Crete and the 1944 Ardennes Offensive proved of limited value in the field.

The Allied advantage in signals intelligence also made it easier to run deception operations, since the enemy's response could be gauged. Both sides at various points attempted, with some success, to deceive enemy aerial reconnaissance through building and deploying dummy tanks, aircraft, and even ships. Both sides also used false radio traffic to try and mislead the enemy about the timing and strength of major operations such as Barbarossa, Sealion,* and Overlord.* Ultra, however, along with greater Allied success in the spy war (most German agents in England, for example, were quickly neutralized or turned into double-agents) meant that the Allies were generally more successful than the Germans and Italians in engaging in large-scale deception operations such as Fortitude* (in which double-agents, false radio traffic and even false radar signals all played a role in convincing the Germans that Operation Overlord, the 1944 Allied invasion of Normandy, was only a feint and that a much larger force would attack across the Pas-de-Calais) [104].

ALLIANCES AND STRATEGY

The Axis

Though the Rome-Berlin diplomatic axis had existed since October 1936, and Fascist Italy and Nazi Germany had been allies in war after June 1940, effective mechanisms for strategic consultation and even operational co-ordination were never properly developed. Mussolini and Hitler attempted to pursue their own war aims while paying as little heed to their nominal ally as possible, and what joint action there was usually arose from Hitler being forced to save Mussolini from the consequences of his own folly. The result was a lack of confidence and growing antipathy, culminating in Italy turning from ally to enemy in the autumn of 1943.

The underlying problem lay in the fact that both dictators wanted to pursue their own goals free of foreign as well as domestic restrictions, while only Germany possessed the material means to do so with real success. Pique over lack of consultation in the crisis of August 1939 combined with envy of German success in 1940 led Mussolini – also without consultation – to pursue goals that were beyond the means of the Italian armed forces. Hence Italian entry into the war against France and Britain in June 1940, and the descent on Greece from Albania at the end of October 1940, though designed to demonstrate Fascist power instead exposed weaknesses that Hitler – to his annoyance – was obliged to rectify.

Though France was already effectively defeated by Germany at the point that Italy entered the war, on the Alpine front French forces brought an Italian offensive to a standstill in the week or so before the Armistice. More humiliations followed, with the Italian air force faring even worse than the *Luftwaffe* in its brief intervention in the

Battle of Britain and the Italian army being pushed back into Libya by British forces in Egypt (after Mussolini had insisted on an offensive which his generals opposed). The invasion of Greece, designed to restore Fascist prestige, turned into another débâcle, with the Greek army throwing Italian forces back into Albania. In no case did Mussolini consult with Hitler about what he intended to do.

These setbacks forced Hitler to act on behalf of his nominal ally in order to secure his southern flank now that the British looked as if they might capitalize on their victories. Hence the German invasion of Greece and Crete and the dispatch to North Africa of what were initially supposed to be just holding forces which soon developed into an Afrika Korps* capable under General Erwin Rommel* of driving the British back into Egypt. In all these operations Italian forces were either ignored completely or made to submit to German command. Though much of the manpower on the Axis side in the Desert War of 1941–42 was Italian, it was the Germans who determined strategy and operational questions. Hitler, for instance, made no attempt to warn Mussolini of his plan to attack Russia, and the Italian forces that Mussolini sent to serve on the Eastern Front were even more subordinate to the German High Command than in Libya.

The enforced nature of Italo-German co-operation only exacerbated suspicion and mutual antipathy at all levels. To the Germans, the Italians were incompetents who had to be propped up; to the Italians, the Germans were overbearing to the point of behaving as overlords rather than allies [Doc. 7]. The events of the summer and autumn of 1943 demonstrated the extent to which each partner regarded the other as a liability to be liquidated. Italian calls for a separate peace with Russia, so that the increasingly precarious Mediterranean front could be shored up, fell on deaf ears. After the overthrow of Mussolini in July 1943 the new Italian government under Marshal Pietro Badoglio* therefore entered secret peace negotiations with the Allies without informing Berlin. The outcome of this was a peace which the Germans pre-empted by occupying the country, brutally incorporating Italian human and other resources into the German war effort, and setting up a puppet regime in the north under Mussolini that was completely subordinate to German wishes. The same pattern of increasing German control was evident with the smaller Axis satellites such as Romania [128].

Thus, from 1941 onward, with increasing obviousness, Axis strategy was essentially German strategy. Moreover, within the Third Reich itself, it was Hitler – and Hitler alone – who increasingly determined both grand strategy and the shape of particular operations.

The process whereby the Führer became supreme warlord as well as head of state can be traced back to 1938 when Hitler had eliminated the posts of War Minister and *Wehrmacht* commander-in-chief (C-in-C). However, in the first years of the war Hitler while dictating general strategy to his generals, had still been willing to modify his designs to meet the practical objections raised by OKW (concerning the need to postpone the attack on France until 1940, for example). The failure of Operation Barbarossa in 1941, however, produced a crisis from which Hitler emerged convinced of his own military genius. Stunned by the Soviet winter counterattack in December 1941–January 1942, the German generals counselled a general retreat. The Führer would have none of it, insisting that all territory taken be held and dismissing those generals he considered weaklings, up to and including the army commander-in-chief. The fact that the front finally stabilized only confirmed Hitler in his belief that he was right. Henceforth all major operational decisions, as well as many minor ones, were made by the Führer, the main theme being the need to hold ground at all costs. If Hitler had been right in the winter of 1941–42 (and this is open to debate) his subsequent decisions were almost uniformly bad. Fixated on offensive action and holding ground at all costs, Hitler refused to listen to contrary advice concerning the merits of strategic defence or the possibility of a separate peace in the East, and went on dismissing generals who were too outspoken. He bears prime responsibility for the disasters that befell the German army on the Eastern Front in 1942–43 (overly ambitious offensives ending in defeat) and in Normandy in 1944 (where refusal to vest control of the Panzer army in the hands of the generals on the spot resulted in crucial time being wasted in responding to the Allied invasion).

On the Axis side, in summary, the key decisions were made by the dictators without mutual consultation and with partial or complete disregard for professional advice. The ultimate result was to hasten total defeat [131].

The Allies

In contrast to the Axis, the British and the Americans managed to develop a close, if not always harmonious, working relationship. Strategic co-ordination with the USSR was more difficult to achieve, but no open rift developed from which Hitler could gain any advantage.

Soviet war strategy, as determined by Stalin, had a single overriding goal: ejecting the Germans from Soviet territory and, more distantly, making sure they posed no future threat. In the first year of the war Stalin made serious errors in refusing to countenance retreat and demanding premature offensives. Subsequently he proved more willing to trust the judgement of proven field commanders such as Zhukov, thereby avoiding at least some of the blunders committed by that other dictator-turned-generalissimo, Hitler. His relations with his Western allies, however, were often strained by diverging interests. To Stalin, the importance of the Allies lay partly in Lend-Lease but mostly in their ability to draw off pressure on the Eastern Front by mounting an offensive in the West (whether successful or not). The repeated postponing of this Second Front, at least as understood by Stalin, generated a great deal of friction – indeed there were times when each side feared that the other would do a deal with Hitler – while both distance and mutual suspicion militated against much co-ordination of Soviet and Anglo–American military action. Indeed, in many respects two parallel but largely separate wars were being waged against Germany. By 1944–45 political differences over the shape of postwar Europe caused a further deterioration in relations (see Chapter 6). The need to defeat the common enemy, however, allowed for competing strategic and political visions to be resolved through compromise or put aside long enough to bring the war to a successful conclusion [127, 130].

The much closer co-ordination of Anglo–American strategy was achieved through a mixture of personal diplomacy at the top and the functioning of an effective joint bureaucracy below. Though there existed serious differences of opinion over a number of key issues, Washington and London were able to form, modify and carry through a true alliance strategy – or series of strategies – for the defeat of the Axis.

As noted above, the United States had begun to move toward active involvement in the war through Lend-Lease and the protection of convoys many months before Hitler officially initiated hostilities. Talks concerning Anglo–American joint action also predated formal US involvement, beginning with a number of secret staff meetings in the first months of 1941 in which the outlines of a joint strategy were sketched. The most central outcome of these talks was the policy of 'Europe First': Germany, rather than Japan, was to be considered the primary threat and dealt with first. These talks were followed by the first summit meeting between Roosevelt and Churchill, who met with their respective chiefs of staff aboard ship at Placentia Bay, Newfoundland, in August 1941 and issued a joint public statement of liberal internationalist principles known as the Atlantic Charter.* The basic principles and overall strategy of the Anglo–American alliance were thus already in place when the United States declared war in December

1941. Actual implementation under war conditions, however, was to prove troublesome.

One problem was that in the wake of Pearl Harbor the Japanese threat loomed much larger in American minds than before (not least that of Admiral Ernest King, the Chief of Naval Operations), while despite the loss of Singapore and Burma in the early part of 1942 the main threat to Britain remained Germany. The principle of defeating Hitler first was adhered to in a new round of staff talks and meetings between Roosevelt and Churchill held between December 1941 and January 1942; but the competing demands on American hearts, minds, and material made by the war against Japan added a new – and potentially divisive – element to joint planning.

The first round of actual joint war planning that took place in early 1942 produced important mechanisms for consultation, particularly the installing of a permanent British staff mission in Washington and the creation of the Combined Chiefs of Staff (CCS*), made up of the chiefs of staff of the services of the two powers. It also revealed differences in how the war ought to be prosecuted. There was agreement among the senior airmen of both nations that a strategic bombing campaign ought to be undertaken and on other matters, but a lack of clear consensus on how the ground war ought to be fought.

In essence, the differences revolved around whether to strike at Germany directly as quickly as possible or to engage in an indirect approach and slowly build up overwhelming force before engaging the *Wehrmacht* head-on. The American generals, led by Chief-of-Staff George C. Marshall,* were strongly in favour of the former (as was Stalin), while the senior British soldiers, represented by Chief of the Imperial General Staff Sir Alan Brooke, inclined towards the latter. Differing memories of the First World War were partly responsible for this, as was the healthy respect the British had developed for German arms since 1940.

Greater British negotiating skill, combined with the relative weakness of American forces and Roosevelt's willingness to be persuaded by Churchill, meant that a cross-Channel attack in 1942 was reluctantly dropped in the spring of that year by the American generals in favour of a build up in England in preparation for a projected 1943 invasion or a possible earlier emergency landing in France. Later in the summer, and with even greater reluctance, Marshall acceded to a plan for an Anglo–American landing in French North Africa towards the end of 1942 which Roosevelt approved for political reasons (a demonstration to the American public on the eve of Congressional elections that the Administration was serious about getting to grips with the enemy on land).

The Allied landings in French North Africa in November 1942 – Operation Torch* – brought to the fore the simmering issue of the political future of France. London had, with varying degrees of enthusiasm, supported de Gaulle's Free French movement since 1940. Washington, however, viewed de Gaulle – inflexible, arrogant, absolutely sure that he was the living embodiment of the true spirit of France – with great suspicion. Viable alternatives, however, proved chimeral. Admiral Jean Darlan, who as Vichy High Commissioner in North Africa had seen which way the wind was blowing and negotiated an armistice with the invading forces in return for American political support, was assassinated by a fanatical resister in December 1942. General Henri Giraud, an escaped POW installed by the Americans as joint head of the French Committee of National Liberation to counterbalance de Gaulle, proved ill-suited to political infighting and was soon neutralized by his rival. By May 1944 de Gaulle had emerged as head of a provisional French government [37].

In the meantime the success of Operation Torch, followed by the clearing of Axis forces from North Africa by early 1943, allowed for the possibility of opening up a major front in the Mediterranean. Churchill and the British strongly supported the idea of a Mediterranean front. This, however, as Marshall pointed out, would drain away some of the men and resources needed for the projected landing in France later that year. Which option to pursue was the main item of debate at the summits held at Casablanca (January 1943), Washington (May 1943), and Quebec (August 1943) attended by Churchill, Roosevelt, and the CCS. Once again, despite serious reservations, Marshall, under orders from Roosevelt, was pressured into accepting first an invasion of Sicily and then a landing in Italy in the late summer of 1943 [129].

The postponement of a 'real' Second Front in Europe in 1943 was bound to be viewed with suspicion in Moscow. Out of ongoing concern that Stalin might negotiate a separate peace with Germany and thus to assure him – and Hitler – that Britain and America were truly committed to a war to the finish, a policy of Unconditional Surrender* was publicly adopted. The phrase, first used by Roosevelt at a press conference after the Casablanca summit, meant that no negotiated peace would be sought: at least not with Nazi Germany. The Allies were committed to the destruction of the Nazi regime as well as the liberation of Occupied Europe [*Doc. 12*].

Meanwhile, where to strike next in the West continued to generate friction between American and British planners. As the Americans were forced to admit, however, British arguments against an invasion of France in 1943, however self-serving, were based on solid evidence. U-boat sinkings and the competing demands of the Pacific War had meant that there was far less shipping available to build up the necessary American forces in Britain in time. Moreover, though Italy proved not to be the 'soft underbelly' that Churchill had imagined, the fighting there did keep German units engaged while giving the Allies time to prepare more fully for the confrontation with the main German forces in the West.

That such a confrontation would finally take place in the spring of 1944 was made clear at the Quebec conference. Despite continuing British desires for more Mediterranean ventures, the relative size of the American war effort and improved negotiating skills were by this time well enough advanced to make sure that Operation Overlord went ahead as scheduled under an American supreme commander, General Dwight Eisenhower.* The last year of the war, in which both the relative and absolute contribution of British forces to the war in Europe shrank, witnessed increasing American dominance in determining strategy. Thus, the American broad-front approach to the invasion of Germany won out over British preference for a narrow thrust and the Mediterranean campaign became a sideshow.

As for the junior allied partners, principally the Dominions and the governments-in-exile based in London, their influence in determining strategy was very limited. Though their contributions to the war were valuable and valued (e.g. Canada, which provided Britain with food and raw materials, aircrew training facilities, as well as contributing significant air, sea, and land forces modelled on their British counterparts to the war effort as the war developed), the smaller allies' strategic interests took second place to those of the major powers. The Polish government in exile, to take a particularly stark example, ultimately found that the desire of London and Washington to come to an accommodation with the Soviet Union meant that their interests were ignored toward the end of the war. The best that the Dominions could do in the way of influencing strategy was to keep their armed forces under their own control as much as possible and determine when and where they should be used.

STRATEGIC BOMBING AND THE U-BOAT WAR

To a large extent the war in Europe revolved around land warfare. As noted, the main bone of contention in Allied strategy from 1942 onwards was where and when ground forces were to break into Occupied Europe and drive back the Wehrmacht. Winning control of the sea and air were necessary preliminaries to a decisive land campaign. On the Eastern Front, a truly continental theatre of operations, non-tactical air and especially naval operations were entirely peripheral. In the West, however, parallel strategies were pursued in which it was hoped that air or naval operations alone might render land campaigns unnecessary.

Strategic Bombing

In the 1920s and 1930s the concept of strategic bombing possessed many admirers within major air forces. Though opinion varied as to how strategic bombing should be carried out – along a spectrum which ran from terrorizing the enemy civilian population by way of saturation bombing of the cities through to destroying key enemy industries by precision bombing of particular factories – the idea that air power alone might so cripple the will or capacity of an enemy as to minimize or even render unnecessary costly land campaigns, held great attraction. In practice, however, it was only the RAF and USAAF that gained enough political and logistical support to put theory into practice in a really sustained manner.

The first wartime attempts at strategic bombing revealed some of the difficulties in turning theory into practice. Disastrous raids by RAF Bomber Command* on heavily defended German ports in 1939 and the high loss rates the *Luftwaffe* sustained over Britain in the summer of 1940 made it clear that prewar assumptions that 'the bomber will always get through' were false. Thus when restraint was abandoned in the autumn of 1940 and strategic attacks were launched against enemy cities, the campaign was conducted at night.

This lowered loss rates, but as both the RAF and the *Luftwaffe* discovered, it also made locating precise targets next to impossible. This helped swing the aims of strategic bombing toward lowering enemy morale through imprecise but heavy bombing of sprawling urban centers which could still, in theory, be located in the dark in a way that an individual factory could not. Neither side, however, achieved much success through strategic bombing in 1940–41. Night navigation made locating even cities difficult, and raids tended to stiffen civilian morale rather than undermine it.

Once the campaign in Russia began in the summer of 1941, German efforts at strategic bombing over Britain slackened off as resources were drawn away from the West (though periodic weak retaliatory campaigns were launched in subsequent years). On the Allied side, meanwhile, strategic bombing, despite its early failures, gained new life.

The revival and massive expansion of the Allied strategic bombing effort from 1942 onward arose from a combination of factors. Both Britain and the United States had few means of striking directly at the enemy other than by air at this point, which made a strategic air campaign still appear attractive. The senior officers of the RAF, such as Bomber Command head Air Chief Marshal Sir Arthur Harris,* as well as Churchill's scientific advisor Professor Lindemann,* moreover, argued that success could be achieved through new navigation aids and production by the thousands of four-engined long-range heavy bombers. If the bomb tonnage dropped on German cities could be significantly raised, then German civilian morale would indeed reach a breaking-point. The senior officers of the USAAF such as 'Hap' Arnold* and Carl Spaatz,* who were also pushing for mass production and deployment to England of four-engine bombers, produced an alternative victory scenario. Lacking the experiences of the RAF in 1939–40, Arnold and his subordinates argued that with enough defensive armament formations of American bombers attacking precise 'bottleneck' industrial targets could achieve success in destroying the German capacity to wage modern industrial war. Both forces were built up in the course of 1942, and in January 1943, after the RAF had already engaged in a number of spectacular 'demonstration' raids involving up to a thousand bombers, both forms of strategic bombing were given a place in Allied strategy at the Casablanca summit and subsequently in the form of a green light for a Combined [in reality separate] Bomber Offensive. Though more traditional strategies would be pursued, the bomber barons would be given a chance to prove their case that bombing could win the war.

The results in 1943 and early 1944 were disappointing. Daylight raids by American bomber formations, mounted deep into German territory, suffered very high losses. The daylight raids mounted against ball bearing facilities at Schweinfurt and Regensburg in August and October 1943 saw over 20 per cent of the bombing force destroyed, and such deep raids had to be suspended [*Doc. 17*]. The limited damage done to German production plant, meanwhile, was quickly repaired. As for the night bombing efforts of the RAF, while aircraft losses were generally lower and the destruction on the ground much greater [*Doc. 16*], the overall effect on German morale and efficiency was not as devastating as was hoped. Under the right weather conditions and with enough aircraft, Bomber Command proved it could wreak enormous havoc in a particular city, as the great firestorm raised in Hamburg one night in July 1943 (40,000 killed) demonstrated. Yet though much damage was done not all German cities proved so vulnerable, as indicated by the high losses (over 5 per cent nightly) and relatively poor effect of the campaign mounted against Berlin in the winter months of 1943–44.

Moreover, successful raids such as Hamburg were matched by disasters such as the attack on Nuremberg in March 1944 in which over 500 aircrew were lost as against 129 Germans. Overall the key problem was that, despite great destruction and the loss of hundreds of thousands of German lives, claims by Harris that Germany was on the verge of collapse proved false. Air raid precautions combined with the tight grip exercised by the Nazi state meant that even after the worst raids civilian morale did not crack to the point of paralysis [*Doc. 15*] [135].

The spring of 1944 did, however, see an improvement in the fortunes of the USAAF. The bombers of the 8th Air Force in Britain were now joined by the bombers of the 15th Air Force in Italy. More importantly, the use of drop tanks meant that American fighters, principally the P-51 Mustang and P-47 Thunderbolt, could escort four-engined B-17 Flying Fortress and B-24 Liberator* bombers all the way to and from targets in Germany. Though bomber losses were still significant, attrition began to take a serious toll on the fighter arm of the *Luftwaffe* [140].

Against the will of the bomber barons the focus of the Anglo–American heavy bomber attacks was partly switched in the spring and summer of 1944 to targets in France, principally railway yards as well as the occasional tactical target. Though rather imprecise, heavy bombers played a significant part in reducing the German capacity to repel the Allied invasion of France in June 1944. Moreover, battles with escort fighters as well as bombers over Germany meant that by this time the *Luftwaffe* had very few fighters to spare to defend airspace over France.

The early summer of 1944 also witnessed the start of the last and most significant German attempt at a retaliatory strategic bombing campaign through the use of missiles. Though technologically in advance of any comparable Allied device, the V-weapons caused consternation but did not materially alter the course of the war. The V-1, essentially an unguided cruise missile, was launched for the most part from fixed sites that could be bombed or overrun in France and later the Low Countries. V-1s could also be shot down by anti-aircraft fire or fast fighters, which meant that only about a third of the 2,452 launched in June 1944 reached London. The more sophisticated V-2, a true ballistic missile that could be launched from a mobile platform and descend on its target at an angle and speed impossible to counter, was a greater menace when attacks on London began in September

1944. Production difficulties and the closing in of Allied armies meant that between May 1944 and March 1945 an average of only three V-2s a day were fired by the Germans: not enough to undermine morale in a really significant manner.

Meanwhile, more Allied success in strategic bombing was achieved over the autumn and winter of 1944–45, as USAAF attacks on the oil industry continued to generate serious shortages of fuel (especially high-grade aviation fuel). Sheer weight of numbers brought on by the Allied superiority in production and training capacity, coupled with advances in navigation and radar jamming techniques, meant that air defences over the Reich at last began to disintegrate. Bomber Command, benefiting from decreased night fighter activity, continued to strike at cities and achieved great success in the Ruhr valley where steel production slumped precipitously in the latter part of 1944. Whether the RAF's destruction of Dresden one night in February 1945, or equally indiscriminate American bombing of Berlin and other cities by day through cloud, materially hastened the end of the war is more questionable.

The record of strategic bombing was thus mixed. Harris and those who thought that civilian morale could be undermined to the point where Germany would collapse were proven wrong, even with over half a million fatal civilian casualties inflicted by the end of the war. Spaatz and the believers in attacks on industry were partially vindicated through the crippling of the German oil and steel industry, but only after severe setbacks and in the context of an improved Allied position as Anglo–American and Russian forces closed in on the Reich. The defeat of the *Luftwaffe* in 1944 was also a major achievement (albeit with considerable help from the Soviet air force over the Eastern Front [134]). Whether or not devoting so much in the way of resources to the strategic bombing was cost effective is more open to debate. Heavy bombers like the Lancaster or Flying Fortress were very sophisticated and thus comparatively expensive weapons requiring a significant proportion of high-end Allied resources, both material and human, to produce and maintain bomber forces of well over a thousand aircraft. The United States was rich enough in every respect to bear this burden well, though the quality of the men in the US army combat arms may have suffered. Britain, however, was already overstretched by 1941, and it is arguable that the massive effort devoted to building up and sustaining the huge Bomber Command fleet in the second half of the war might have been more cost effective if at least a portion of the resources had been devoted to, say, improving the poor quality and limited quantity of British army vehicles.

The U-Boat War

Air bombardment was not the only alternative means of winning the war pursued by either side in the West. There were also efforts to strike decisively at the enemy economy through blockade at sea. The extent of German conquests on land in 1940–42, coupled with the development of a range of substitutes for imported materials such as rubber, made the British surface blockade of German ports less effective than it had been in the First World War. Meanwhile German submarines, in what became known as the Battle of the Atlantic, were mounting a campaign to sink Allied shipping which at times appeared to be on the verge of preventing enough food and other resources from reaching Britain and thus forcing the British to sue for peace [146].

The relative weakness of the German surface fleet compared with the Royal Navy meant that the weight on any campaign against Allied shipping would inevitably have to be borne by vessels easily able to evade visual detection: the U-boats. The campaign really began only when the geographical constrictions of vessels operating only from German ports were overcome with the conquest of Norway, France and the Low Countries in 1940. This caused the German Naval High Command to conclude that a chance now existed for the German navy to win the war by severing Britain's vital maritime communications.

This first phase of the Battle of the Atlantic, however, in 1940–41, proved to be a failure. The vulnerability of single surface raiders to British squadrons, already evident with the destruction of the pocket battleship *Graf Spee* in 1939, was demonstrated conclusively with the sinking of the battleship *Bismarck* in May 1941. As for the U-boats, there were only about twenty available over the winter of 1940–41, as against the 300 the U-boat fleet commander, Vice-Admiral Karl Dönitz,* had calculated were necessary for absolute success.

Nevertheless the U-boats that were operational at this time scored some successes through innovative 'Wolf Pack'* tactics. Patrol lines were established in the Atlantic to maximize the chances of spotting a merchant convoy. Once a U-boat (or a long range reconnaissance aircraft) had made visual contact, the other U-boats would be informed by radio and would converge on the convoy being trailed, the wolf pack using darkness and numbers to confuse the few defending escort vessels when the moment arrived to fire torpedoes. Under optimum conditions the results could be devastating, as when two eastbound convoys in late October 1940 lost a total of thirty-three out of seventy-nine merchant ships.

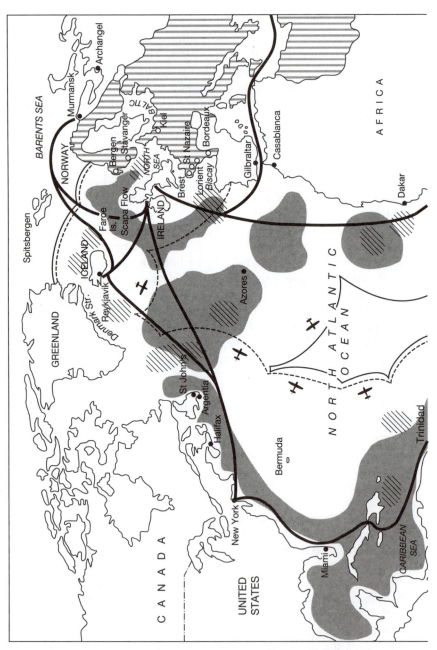

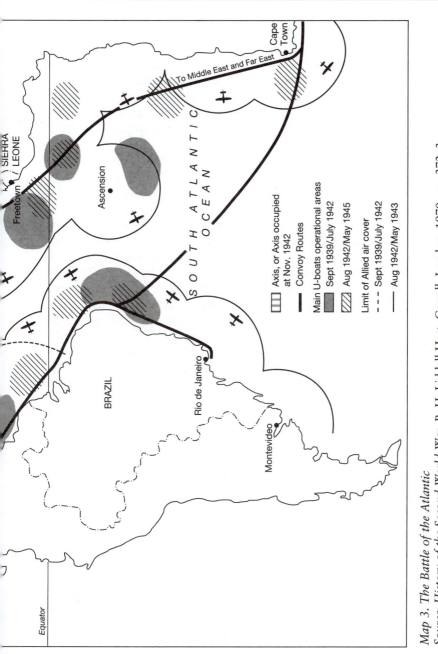

Map 3. The Battle of the Atlantic
Source: History of the Second World War, B. H. Liddell Hart, Cassell, London, 1970, pp. 372–3

Though the establishment of escort bases in Iceland and New-foundland helped extend the range of escort vessels and air cover, and US navy (USN*) escorts took up some of the strain in the Western Atlantic in the autumn of 1941, Royal Navy and Royal Canadian Navy (RCN*) destroyers and corvettes were not numerous enough and lacked an effective radar capable of spotting surfaced U-boats beyond visual range. Overall, however, the small size of the U-boat fleet in 1940–41 meant that shipping tonnage sunk could be made up through new construction.

1942 began well for the U-boats as a flawed USN policy of aggressive patrolling and no inshore convoys gave the submariners easy pickings off the American coast until the policy was abandoned in the summer [*Doc. 18*]. Moreover, in 1942 the number of U-boats being built exceeded sinkings while the reverse was true of British shipbuilding; and German signals intelligence was having more success than the British in anticipating enemy movements. Convoys, especially slow convoys, became easier targets. In November 1942 over 725,000 tons of Allied shipping was sunk; a figure which, if it could be sustained, Dönitz calculated would cut the Allied lifeline across the Atlantic. The huge shipbuilding capacity of the United States made this a dubious assumption, but there was no doubt that in 1942–43 U-boats were doing harm to Allied efforts to build up strength in England for operations in Europe. In March 1943 a new low was reached when two eastbound convoys without enough escorts were savaged by a pack of forty U-boats, twenty-three out of ninety-two merchant ships being lost at the cost of a single U-boat [139].

Therefore 1943 looked to be a good year for the submarine campaign, if only in seriously delaying the build up for the cross-Channel invasion. In fact 1943 turned out to be the year of decisive defeat for the U-boats. Even with sixty U-boats operating in the Atlantic by the spring of 1943, a greater number of escorts, new technology, and greater co-ordination, coupled with the huge merchant tonnage the USA would build, brought about defeat.

Success in decoding enemy signals was by now about evenly split between the British and the Germans, but in actual battle the U-boats began to suffer serious losses. New centimetric radar, mounted on very long-range aircraft (many also by now equipped with a powerful searchlight) and an increasing number of surface escort vessels, made surfaced U-boats much more vulnerable to detection and pre-emptive attack both day and night, as did high-frequency direction finding equipment (HF/DF) that allowed escorts to locate U-boats when they sent radio signals. Forward-fired depth charges also allowed escort vessels to maintain sonar contact during attacks on submerged U-boats, while the strength of convoy air cover was increased through the deployment of small new escort aircraft carriers. Many of these improvements dated from the latter part of 1942 or even earlier, but it was only in the summer of 1943 that experience in their use and the full range of improvements began to tell decisively.

Thus, though plenty of merchant ships were still being sunk, the U-boats themselves suddenly began to disappear in large numbers; the hunters having themselves landed among the hunted. No less than thirty-three U-boats were sunk by the British, Canadians, and Americans in May 1943, mostly in the North Atlantic. Dönitz switched his emphasis to the mid-Atlantic, only to find the USN ready and waiting. In July 1943, twenty-two more U-boats were sunk by USN air and surface escorts. The monthly tonnage of merchant shipping declined to five figure totals, a loss rate that was more than made up for by the massive increase in US merchant shipping production. Though U-boats continued to operate and sink ships until the last days of the war, they no longer posed a threat to either British survival or the Allied capacity to mount operations against Europe from England. Allied success on land and in the air meant that the new types of U-boat, that might have reversed the balance in favour of the submariners, did not arrive in time [144].

The U-boat campaign, therefore, ultimately failed either to bring Britain to its knees or seriously impede the arrival of men and material from North America needed to carry the war to the Continent. That in turn meant that by 1943–44 the *Wehrmacht* had to face the prospect of invasion from the West at a time when its fortunes on the Eastern Front were going from bad to worse.

5   THE EBB OF *BLITZKRIEG*, 1942–45

THE CHANGING BALANCE OF FORTUNE, 1942–43

Though both the air campaign in the West and the U-boat war were escalating in 1942 and early 1943, it was the war on land in the East that consumed most German attention and resources in this period. Once more Hitler would seek to cripple the Soviet Union, and once more – this time definitively – he would be thwarted by the strength and resilience of the Red Army. In North Africa, meanwhile, the Allies would at last manage to defeat Axis forces decisively.

The Mediterranean

Though small scale in comparison with the titanic Russo-German struggle in the east, the outcome of the war in the south between Axis and Allied forces was of considerable significance. If the Afrika Korps and Italian forces under Rommel could decisively defeat the 8th Army in North Africa and drive the British from Egypt, then the entire Middle East and its oil resources would be imperilled. There was even talk of German forces in Russia driving south from the Caucasus and the Afrika Korps driving north through the Middle East to link up in Iraq or Iran. Conversely, if the Axis could be defeated in the Mediterranean and driven out of North Africa entirely the Allies would be in a position to follow on with possible landings anywhere from Greece to Southern France: Italy would itself become vulnerable to invasion.

Which side realized its dreams concerning the Mediterranean world would, first of all, depend on the outcome of the campaigns fought in North Africa in 1942. This outcome in turn depended to a considerable degree on each side's ability to supply or augment the forces fighting there. Though code breaking, leadership, equipment, and training all played their part, logistics played a particularly crucial part in the Desert War.

The year 1942 began inauspiciously for the British in North Africa. It was true that starting in November of 1941, after a series of stalled offensives earlier in the year, the 8th Army under the overall command of General Claude Auchinleck,* had pushed the Afrika Korps several hundred miles into Libya. This victory, however, was based, in part, on success in intercepting enemy supply convoys at sea. Increased German air and submarine support in the Mediterranean, coupled with some Italian naval successes, meant that by the end of the year it was British rather than Axis convoys that were not getting through. Rommel's worn-down forces in Libya were replenished, and in January and May 1942 new Axis offensives succeeded in defeating the 8th Army – less adept in co-ordinating the action of its armour, artillery, and infantry than the Afrika Korps – and driving it back into Egypt as far as El Alamein.

Rommel seemed poised to drive on to Cairo and beyond; yet even as the British were being driven back in early 1942, the logistical balance was beginning to swing against the Axis. This was, in part, the inevitable result of the stretching and contraction of supply lines that each side experienced as the result of successful desert offensives. The enemy would be driven back hundreds of miles, the pursuers getting farther from their key supply ports on the one hand and the retreating defenders closer to theirs on the other. The shifting balance was also the result of Britain's success in reinforcing the island of Malta in the central Mediterranean, signals intelligence, and concurrent success in preventing much fuel and other critical supplies from reaching Rommel through air and sea attacks.

Hence when the Afrika Korps launched renewed attacks in July, and again in late August 1942, the 8th Army was strong enough to prevent a renewed Axis drive into Egypt. In subsequent months the strength of the 8th Army was built up even further. The German and Italian divisions, meanwhile, proved more difficult to reinforce. The result was that when the 8th Army, under the command of General Bernard Montgomery* since August, went over to the attack again on 23 October 1942, it possessed numerical superiority in almost every category of equipment and an almost five-to-one superiority in tanks. Starved of fuel and replacements, the Afrika Korps (despite heavy fighting [*Doc. 19*]) was unable to withstand the blow, and though Rommel was able to extricate his more mobile units before they could be encircled along with the Italians, a full retreat across Libya began [147].

The change in fortune brought about by this Third Battle of El Alamein, in which Axis forces had been defeated through weight of firepower more than through superior generalship, turned out to be definitive. Even as the Afrika Korps was retreating westwards in disarray, combined Anglo-American forces were landing in French Morocco and Algeria in November 1942, creating a new Allied Front to the rear.

The ambivalence of the Vichy government in France over whether to support the Allies or the Axis at this point allowed the Germans to despatch troops over to Tunisia to act as a blocking force, and the advance by the 8th Army from Libya and the 1st Army from Algeria was bitterly contested over the winter of 1942–43 by Rommel and General von Arnim.* Despite operational setbacks, however, the Allies could reinforce their units far more effectively now than the enemy, who were now relying heavily on a vulnerable air supply route. In April 1943, when the general advance was renewed, the German and Italian defences collapsed. Though it had taken longer than expected, the Axis had finally been driven from the southern half of the Mediterranean, leaving behind 238,000 prisoners of war on top of the 30,000 already captured in the wake of El Alamein [149].

Russia

Meanwhile, on the Eastern Front, an even more significant reversal of fortune had occurred. Here again logistical factors, and in particular the comparative ability of each side to make good losses in men and material, would play a key part in determining success or failure.

The early months of 1942 had seen a recovery of German fortunes in Russia. In May, a poorly co-ordinated Soviet counteroffensive towards Kharkov led by Marshal Timoshenko* had led to yet another encirclement battle in which over 300,000 Red Army troops became casualties, leaving the forces facing what would be the main German thrust of 1942 severely weakened. Hitler, meanwhile, had been directing plans for a renewed German drive eastward in the summer. This time the advance would be by Army Group South alone, the aim being to drive to the Volga and thrust down into the Caucasus, depriving the USSR of much of its industry and oil resources. If it worked – and the Soviet disaster at Kharkov had increased the odds in the *Wehrmacht*'s favour – Operation 'Blue'* would do what Operation Barbarossa had failed to achieve: the crippling of the Soviet capacity to wage modern war.

Initially, the main German offensive of 1942 on the Eastern Front, launched at the end of June, seemed to be a repeat of the great victories of the previous year. Stalin was deceived into thinking the main thrust would be in the centre against Moscow, Soviet defences in the south were broken through, and the Panzers lunged eastwards to begin a series of encirclements. By August the Crimea had been cleared, the

Lower Don river had been crossed and Army Group A was rapidly advancing toward the Caucasus while Army Group B reached out towards the Volga and the city of Stalingrad. Once more it looked as if the Soviet Union was on the brink of defeat.

There were signs, however, that the *Wehrmacht* was overextending its resources and that the Red Army still had plenty of muscle. For the first time Stalin had allowed Red Army commanders to retreat, which meant that the Panzer encirclements yielded only modest numbers of killed and captured Soviet troops. Soviet manpower reserves and industrial output allowed for new armies to be created and equipped to defend the line of the Volga. Meanwhile, the limits of German resources meant only a thrust in one sector could be contemplated. Fewer Panzers were available, and more low-quality Axis satellite divisions (Romanian, Hungarian and Italian) had to be used to protect the line of advance by Army Group B than the *Wehrmacht* generals would have liked.

By September 1942 the Germans had reached their limit at Stalingrad. A city reduced to ruin by air and artillery bombardment, Stalingrad was bitterly contested by Soviet and German formations in the following weeks. Though the German 6th Army under Freidrich von Paulus* eventually took most of the city as winter closed in, it was at the tip of a dangerously exposed salient stretching back hundreds of miles. In November 1942 the Red Army launched a two-pronged counterattack, Operation Uranus,* that aimed to pinch off the salient and surround the 6th Army in Stalingrad. Three well-equipped Soviet armies fell on underequipped Romanian forces and understrength Panzer divisions, and within days the 6th Army found itself cut off. Hitler once more refused to contemplate retreat. Efforts to supply the beleaguered Germans in Stalingrad by air proved inadequate, and a relief thrust by three understrength Panzer divisions failed to break the Soviet stranglehold. An already desperate situation was made worse in mid-December 1942 when new Soviet offensives (Southwest Front) caused the disintegration of the 8th Italian, 2nd Hungarian, and 3rd Romanian armies, as well as severely mauling German forces. Though most of the *Wehrmacht* forces in the Caucasus were extricated before they could be cut off, the 6th Army's fate was sealed [*Doc. 8*]. On 1 February 1943 the Battle of Stalingrad ended with von Paulus surrendering what was left of his command. The news sent shock waves through Germany. On top of the 150,000 Germans killed at Stalingrad another 30,000 were taken prisoner [151].

Though a series of well-planned and brilliantly executed counterattacks in the early months of 1943 by Manstein kept defeat from turning into utter rout, there was no question that the Germans had suffered an unmitigated disaster. The balance of power in the East was now swinging irrevocably in favour of the Soviets as mobilization of human resources accelerated and war production increased at a time when the Germans were losing men and material that could not be replaced on the same scale. In addition the Red Army was proving that it had learned from previous mistakes and could organize truly effective offensives against an enemy whose supreme commander showed an increasing unwillingness to listen to professional advice. Like the Axis defeat in North Africa, though on a vastly greater and more significant scale, the disaster at Stalingrad indicated that the tide was finally turning decisively against the Axis powers in Europe [*Doc. 20*] [150].

SUCCESS AND FAILURE SOUTH AND EAST, 1943–44

The Italian Campaign

Imminent Allied success in Tunisia opened up the possibility of launching a major offensive against the Axis across the Mediterranean. After the usual Anglo-American disagreements had been smoothed over at the Casablanca summit, it was agreed that Sicily should be invaded by airborne and amphibious landings in July 1943 (Operation Husky*). Though it ended in Allied victory, Operation Husky suggested that moving across the Mediterranean did not constitute, as Churchill had opined, a blow against a soft underbelly. A mixture of bad luck and friction between Montgomery (commanding the British 8th Army) and General George Patton* (commanding the American 7th Army) resulted in poor co-ordination of Anglo-American forces. German forces in Sicily, though unable to launch successful counterattacks, fought hard [*Doc. 21*] and were able to carry out an effective fighting retreat. Over 100,000 men (40,000 of them German troops) and much equipment were ferried across the straits of Messina onto the Italian mainland in August before they could be cut off or interdicted by Allied forces [153].

Though they helped bring about the collapse of Italian resistance, the subsequent Anglo-American amphibious landings on the Italian mainland in September 1943 proved to be hard-fought operational successes from which no immediate strategic advantage accrued. German Army Group C under the able Field Marshal Albert Kesselring,* aided by mountainous terrain and river lines ideal for defence, fought a series of bitter attritional engagements – the early battles for

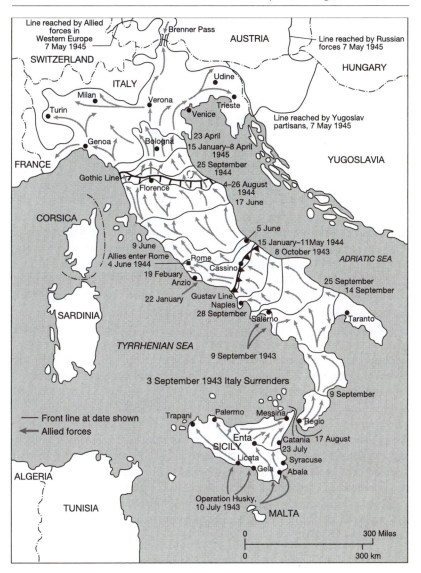

Map 4. The Italian Campaign
Source: The Second World War, John Keegan, Hutchinson, London, 1989,
p. 355

Cassino being among the most notorious – that bogged down the Allied advance south of Rome in the winter of 1943–44. Indifferent Allied generalship, notably that of Mark Clark* (commanding the 5th US Army), did not improve matters. An attempt to envelop the Gustav Line,* the main German defensive position, by making another amphibious landing at Anzio in January 1944, only reinforced the stalemate: a sluggish Allied advance being contained through a swift German counterattack [152].

Though possessing a clear superiority both on the ground and (especially) in the air, the Allies were not able to pierce the Gustav Line successfully until May 1944. Though Rome fell in June, a combination of poor Allied generalship, good defensive terrain, and the switching of Allied resources to the campaign in France meant that the subsequent advance into northern Italy was both slow and costly. The campaign to break through the Gothic Line* defences in the autumn of 1944 and winter of 1944–45 was yet another attritional slogging match, and only at the end of April 1945 did Kesselring finally surrender. Mussolini, meanwhile, trying to flee to Switzerland, was caught and shot by Italian partisans [155].

In operational terms, therefore, the Italian campaign was a greater success for the Germans than for the Allies. It also generated a good deal of Anglo-American friction. The campaign did, however, tie down over twenty German divisions in Italy and dozens of other divisions in parts of southeast Europe (placed to anticipate further Allied amphibious landings) which might otherwise have been used to try and stem the Russian tide or reinforce the German defences in France. By the winter of 1943–44, conversely, though there was much bickering over the allocation of resources such as landing craft, the British (whose armies were at their zenith in terms of size) together with the Americans (whose armed forces were still expanding) were able to wage the campaign while also building up forces for the cross-Channel invasion of France (albeit more slowly than Marshall and Stalin would have liked).

The Eastern Front

Though the *Wehrmacht* had been severely weakened by the Stalingrad disaster, Hitler rejected the advice of Manstein and others that it conduct a mobile, fluid defence in 1943 as a means of conserving resources while wearing down the enemy. Though the scope would have to be more limited than in 1941 or 1942, the Führer insisted on a summer offensive (Operation Citadel*). New tank models, it was hoped, would ensure the success of a two-pronged encirclement of the

Soviet-held salient at Kursk, between Army Group Centre and Army Group South, which would lead to the destruction of the Soviet armies within it as well as shortening the German front line.

The Battle of Kursk, fought in July of 1943, was yet another indication that in the second half of the war the dazzling successes of *Blitzkrieg* were giving way to an attritional struggle in which brute force counted for as much or more than operational or tactical subtlety. The general staff of the Red Army (Stavka*) had learned from its mistakes, and knew that a mixture of timely retreats, in-depth field defences, and well-planned offensives in superior force could blunt the German sword and drive back the *Wehrmacht* [*Doc. 9*]. It also helped immensely that intelligence from the British and other sources allowed Stalin to anticipate correctly where the blow would fall. Defences within the Kursk salient were deepened and strengthened and a reserve of six armies was built up. The result was that when the 700,000 troops and 2,400 tanks and self-propelled guns of the German 9th army and 4th Panzer army attacked from north and south respectively, they ran into over a million Soviet troops and 3,400 Soviet tanks and self-propelled guns. The Soviets could also deploy more combat aircraft. The resulting clash produced the greatest tank battle in history; and ended in a singular German defeat. Though some advances were made and Soviet forces suffered heavy losses, the German pincers were steadily weakened and unable to close. Within two weeks the offensive was aborted.

Even before Operation Citadel had collapsed the Red Army had begun to launch its own summer offensives, first striking at the Orel salient north of the Kursk battle and eliminating it and then in August 1943 striking towards Kharkov to the south. The relative sophistication of Red Army operational planning by this point, and above all the sheer strength of the forces involved, meant the defeat of counter-attacks by already weakened Panzer forces that had been hurried to the danger zone. A Soviet general offensive followed and, after some initial setbacks, the Red Army forced the *Wehrmacht* into headlong retreat towards the Dnieper river in September 1943, along which the front congealed as the winter set in. The subsequent winter offensive launched by the Red Army resulted, by March 1944, in the total reconquest of the Ukraine. Soviet numerical superiority and operational effectiveness in dealing with German counterstrokes, combined with Hitler's usual insistence on holding ground, led to the liberation of hundreds of square miles of Soviet territory and hundreds of thousands of enemy casualties. Winter efforts in the centre and north were less successful, though moves to relieve Leningrad did drive Army

Group North southwestward some 200 miles. By the spring the initiative on the Eastern Front lay definitively with the Red Army [154].

CLOSING THE RING, 1944–45

By early 1944 it was clear to all that the tide of war was flowing fast against Nazi Germany. Despite great increases in war production and manpower mobilization, as well as some impressive performances by the *Wehrmacht* and *Waffen-SS* in defensive operations, the Reich simply could not match the combined capacities of its adversaries (in particular the USA and USSR). Germany still, however, possessed certain advantages which, if they could be exploited, could postpone the day of reckoning and possibly even create the conditions for a negotiated armistice. Much depended on whether or not the long anticipated Allied cross-Channel invasion of France – long in preparation and finally coming to fruition – could be repulsed. If the invasion were defeated, then many of the units currently deployed in the West along the so-called 'Atlantic Wall'* could be sent to reinforce the Eastern Front. A resounding victory might lead the Allies to reconsider their aim of Unconditional Surrender and make Stalin consider anew a separate peace with Germany.

Moreover the odds of German success in the West seemed high. Though they possessed near-total command of the air and sea on and over the Channel and over western France, the Allies were faced with the task of carrying out an amphibious invasion along the most heavily defended coastline in Europe. There were nearly sixty German divisions manning the Atlantic Wall or in reserve in France (a quarter of them of very high quality), and gun emplacements, pillboxes, mines, barbed wire and other obstacles abounded, the result of two years' work preparing for such an attack. Wherever the landing took place, therefore, it would be contested from the moment landing craft were spotted. Even if invasion troops successfully established themselves ashore, they would have to face counterattacks by Panzer and other mobile units being held in reserve before they had a chance to build up a superiority in tanks and heavy weapons. Eisenhower, the American general given supreme command of the Allied invasion force, knew full well that even with the best plans possible, Operation Overlord would be a major gamble.

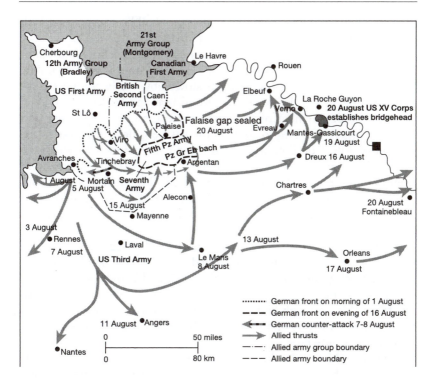

Map 5. The Normandy breakout
Source: *The Second World War,* John Keegan, Hutchinson, London, 1989, p. 406.

The Advance from the West

Allied preparations for Overlord, the biggest amphibious operation ever, were meticulous and extensive. Special equipment and techniques were developed, command of the English Channel established at sea and in the air, railway yards and other communication hubs in France were systematically bombed, and elaborate and successful measures taken to deceive the enemy as to the location and nature of the Allied landings. Nothing was left to chance, but how well the operation would go in reality remained to be seen.

D-day, the start of the Allied invasion of Europe, began early on 6 June when 23,000 British and American airborne troops landed in Normandy in anticipation of a five-division beach assault by over 130,000 British, American and Canadian troops a few hours later. Though there were serious difficulties with one of the American landings, by nightfall the German beach defences had been overcome with much lighter Allied casualties than anticipated.

Now that the Allies were successfully established ashore and building up their forces, a counterattack by Army Group B was inevitable. The German response, however, was slowed by overly complex command arrangements (Rommel, von Rundstedt and Hitler all having a hand in the deployment of armoured forces), an ongoing belief that the main attack was still to come in the Pas-de-Calais (a tribute to the success of Allied deception measures), and the manner in which the French Resistance and Allied bombing hindered the movement of armoured reserves to Normandy. This allowed the Allies time to consolidate their hold and push inland twenty miles or so in the face of only uncoordinated and sporadic counterattacks over the next few weeks.

By July 1944, however, a stalemate seemed to be setting in. The expansion of the bridgehead and Allied forces in Normandy was progressing much more slowly than anticipated, and despite Allied control of the air – which made road movement in daylight extremely hazardous [*Doc. 24*] – enough high-quality German forces were reaching the front to blunt various offensive drives by Allied ground forces.

The Allies, however, could replace their losses in a manner that the Germans could not. In the last week of July, American forces in the south were able to punch successfully through the German cordon while the majority of the German armoured forces were tied down fighting the British and Canadians further north. Hitler's insistence in early August 1944 on a full-scale counterattack rather than withdrawal to more defensible positions in response to this development led to the destruction of most of what remained of the German armour and exposed the German forces in Normandy to possible envelopment between American forces swinging up from the south and British and Canadian forces pushing southward. Hitler finally gave the order to retreat on 16 August, and though many Germans escaped from the Falaise pocket before it closed on 19 August, it was clear that German combat power had been destroyed. The Allies had won the battle for Normandy, another major landing on the French Riviera starting on 15 August had opened up a new and virtually unopposed front in the south, and the remnants of Army Group B were in headlong flight [157].

For a time it looked as if the war might end in 1944 as the US 3rd Army under General Patton as well as other Allied formations in the 12th and 21st Army Groups rapidly fanned out across France and Belgium, denying the enemy an opportunity to form a new defensive line of any substance. There were, however, limits to what could be accomplished. Allied logistical constraints, Anglo-American disagreement as to how to go about driving into Germany, and the partial recovery of enemy strength combined to make a 1945 campaign necessary.

The central difficulty militating against an Allied offensive into Germany in the autumn of 1944 was the fact that the majority of supplies, not least fuel and ammunition, came by sea via a narrow funnel in Normandy and then all the way across France. Other than Cherbourg no major port in operational condition was in Allied hands by this point, transporting material across the beaches was plagued with difficulties, and the destruction of the railway network meant that the large – but by no means unlimited – Anglo-American truck fleet was largely responsible for transshipment. With limited available resources, serious Anglo-American friction arose over operational priorities. Montgomery (not the most tactful of British commanders) wanted American units to be placed under his command so that they could support a northern thrust through the Netherlands and down into the Ruhr valley by his 21st Army Group. Neither General Omar Bradley* (commanding 12th Army Group) nor Patton (who wanted to push his 3rd US Army toward Frankfurt) liked this idea, and after much acrimony Eisenhower came down in favour of a broad-front advance once logistical constraints had been solved by the opening up of Marseilles and Antwerp to Allied shipping.

That Eisenhower was probably right to be cautious about Montgomery's plan for a knock-out blow before winter set in was demonstrated by the more limited operation that he did allow to go forward in September 1944. Montgomery's plan was to try and outflank the prewar Siegfried Line and establish a bridgehead for further operations by using three airborne divisions (two American and one British) to seize key bridges across Holland as far as the lower Rhine at Arnhem (Operation Market-Garden*). The result was a disaster. German forces in the area were much stronger than anticipated, and British ground forces were unable to advance quickly enough to prevent airborne troops from being driven from the key bridge at Arnhem. The operation also diverted attention from the opening of the Scheldt Estuary and delayed the opening of Antwerp to shipping until November 1944.

A further and more alarming indication that the *Wehrmacht* still possessed much fighting power came in mid-December when Hitler, having marshalled his dwindling resources in men and material, launched a surprise offensive with twelve Panzer divisions in the thinly held Ardennes sector. The hope was to repeat the success of 1940 by driving towards Antwerp, cutting the northern Allied armies off from their supply base. Despite initial German success, however, the Allies recovered rapidly and managed to contain the enemy advance in what became known as the Battle of the Bulge. The Allied forces were more mobile than the German army by this point and despite Anglo-American friction were able to rush units to critical points in time. Once the weather cleared on 23 December, Allied air superiority once more made itself felt. By Christmas Day the German advance, already in trouble, had ground to a halt. In January the remaining German units were withdrawn from the bulge.

Having built up his forces (the number of American troops in particular having increased significantly) and recovered from the Ardennes surprise, Eisenhower in the new year contemplated how best to invade the Reich. Montgomery, predictably, wanted all efforts to be subordinated to a thrust by his 21st Army Group. Equally predictably this was not an idea that won applause from American generals. Eisenhower decided in favour of a general advance to the Rhine, the establishment of bridgeheads, and then the envelopment of the Ruhr from north and south. A single massive thrust in the north could not be supported.

The Rhineland campaign ran from February through to the third week of March 1945, German units in the north putting up particularly strong opposition to the advance of the 2nd British, 1st Canadian, and 9th US armies. The result, however, was to put the Allies in a position to throw bridgeheads across the Rhine in the last fortnight of March (with the support of Bomber Command and airborne landings) and then place the 1st US Army and the 9th US Army in a position to surround what remained of German Army Group B in the Ruhr pocket (where over 300,000 soldiers surrendered in April).

Interpretation of the last phase of the 1945 campaign in the West is conditioned by knowledge of the postwar division of Europe into competing spheres. Eisenhower, in March 1945, was more concerned with military than political considerations, which was why he saw a thrust southwestward, towards what was assumed to be the locale of a Nazi last stand in a redoubt amidst the Bavarian and Austrian Alps, rather than directly eastward towards Berlin, as the primary axis of advance. Allied movement eastward did still continue, however: the 2nd British army cleared the north German coast and the 9th and 1st US armies advanced toward the Elbe and Mulde rivers where they met up with Soviet forces. Organized German resistance in the West collapsed in late April. The Nazi redoubt in the southeast proved to

Map 6. The Red Army moves West, 1944–45
Source: The Second World War, John Keegan, Hutchinson, London, 1989,
p. 503

be a mirage, and it was the Red Army rather than the Allies who took
Berlin at the end of the month. Political considerations urged on him
by London and Washington did, however, move Eisenhower to focus
on the British advance toward Lübeck in the north so as to secure the
approaches to Denmark in the first days of May before the Soviets
could get there. With nearly all Germany occupied and in ruins, the
German armies finally surrendered, a general Unconditional Surrender document being signed on 7 May 1945 [163].

The Advance from the East

Even as the preparations for Overlord were being finalized in the first
months of 1944, Stavka was drawing up plans for a summer offensive
in the East. Through bitter experience Stalin had learned to avoid

overly grandiose expectations, and Marshals Zhukov* and Alexander Vasilievsky* were allowed to orchestrate the summer campaign in line with logistical limitations. The aim of Operation Bagration* was, nevertheless, considerable in scope: the elimination of the 300-mile deep salient in Belorussia north of the Pripet marshes defended by Army Group Centre. If successful, five well-planned offensives would cut off Army Group North, free the remaining territory of the USSR in German hands, and open up a route through Poland towards Berlin.

The salient was in some respects an obvious target, Hitler having refused requests that the army be allowed to withdraw to a less vulnerable line of defence. Soviet deception measures designed to focus German attention on the south, however, meant that when the main offensive began on 22 June 1944, Army Group Centre was both weakened by transfers elsewhere and taken completely by surprise. The concentration of forces meant that the Red Army enjoyed overwhelming superiority in men and material, and Army Group Centre was shattered in a series of encirclements. Successive hammer blows in the centre and then follow-up advances north into the Baltic states and Leningrad region and south into the Balkans shattered sixty German divisions and generated over 460,000 enemy casualties. By the time logistical strains and stiffening resistance had brought the offensives to a halt in the autumn, both Romania and Finland had signed an armistice, Bulgaria had been occupied, and the Red Army was on the East Prussian border and deep into Hitler's remaining satellite, Hungary [161].

Even at this stage in the war the Germans proved dangerous opponents. Skilful enemy commanders such as Field Marshal Walther Model,* known as the Führer's Fireman, managed to reorganize shattered units and extract a high price in Red Army men and material for ground gained through well-organized counterattacks [156].

At the end of 1944 the Red Army at last began to suffer from a serious manpower shortage, the crisis being especially acute in infantry units. The German manpower situation was however even more acute, and the war production of the USSR meant that manpower at the front could be made up for by greater concentrations of firepower (artillery, tanks, self-propelled guns and ground-attack aircraft) and using women in front-line combat roles.

In January 1945, with Hitler's attention and many of the remaining *Waffen-SS* and *Wehrmacht* mobile reserves fixed on the Soviet threat in Hungary, a new Red Army offensive began in Poland. Once again overwhelming superiority of force had been concentrated and, aided by Hitler's micromanagement of German forces and insistence on no retreat, the Red Army advanced 300 miles to establish bridge-heads over the Oder river by the time logistical strains called a halt in February. Combined with the Allied occupation of the Ruhr, the overrunning of Poland (where many factories had been set up beyond the range of Allied bombers) deprived the Reich of what remained of its war production capacity [158].

With Berlin now directly threatened, Hitler and OKW struggled to assemble a credible defence along the Oder-Neisse river line in February and March 1945. By stripping the forces in the West to the bone and mobilizing old men and boys in a people's militia (*Volkssturm**), a force of nearly one million men equipped with small arms and effective short-range anti-tank weapons and supported by anti-aircraft artillery and what remained of the Panzer arm was deployed in successive belts on the approaches to the capital. Atrocities by an avenging Red Army in East Prussia and elsewhere gave the defenders the strength of desperation, the hope being that the communist hordes could be held off long enough for most of Germany to be occupied by the Western Allies. And even if no 'arrangement' could be made with the British and Americans to join in defending European civilization from the ravages of Asiatic-communist barbarism, then Hitler himself was quite prepared to see what remained of Germany utterly destroyed rather than surrender.

Knowledge of German hopes accelerated Soviet preparations for a thrust towards Berlin, but it was not until mid-April 1945 that sufficient forces had been concentrated by Marshals Zhukov, Konev*, and Konstantin Rokossovksy* to allow the attackers an over two-to-one advantage in manpower, a four-to-one advantage in tanks and self-propelled guns, and a nearly five-to-one advantage in artillery. The battle for Berlin was a savage and drawn-out affair, with the Germans skilfully and desperately contesting every yard of ground. Nevertheless by 25 April the city had been surrounded, and over the next seven days Red Army troops fought their way into Berlin street by street. Surrounded and powerless, Hitler shot himself on 30 April, leaving the Berlin garrison commander to surrender on 2 May. A general unconditional capitulation was arranged the following week, Eisenhower rebuffing efforts by Grand Admiral Dönitz, Hitler's designated successor, to negotiate a surrender only to the Western Allies. On 8 May 1945, with Anglo-American and Russian forces meeting and greeting one another at the Elbe on the ruins of the Third Reich, the second of two general surrender documents was signed in Berlin at Soviet insistence. VE Day dawned amid general rejoicing in the West. Though Soviet operations in the Prague area continued for another few days, the Second World War in Europe had finally come to an end [160].

PART THREE: ASSESSMENT

6 THE END OF THE WAR AND AFTER

COSTS AND THE DIVISION OF EUROPE

For all sides save the United States, the Second World War was the most devastating conflict of modern times. At least 36 million people lost their lives between 1939 and 1945 in Europe, roughly three times the figure for the First World War. Moreover, the majority of those who died were civilians (approximately 23 million), a sobering indication of the way in which total war had blurred distinctions between combatants and non-combatants. In line with the exceptional scale and savagery of the war in Eastern Europe, the bulk of both military and civilian casualties occurred in this theatre. Over 13 million Soviet and over 3 million German soldiers (as well as over a million Finnish, Italian, Hungarian, and Romanian servicemen combined) died fighting on the Eastern Front or in captivity. In those states which succumbed to *Blitzkrieg*, military casualties were often relatively small, but under the savage conditions of German or Soviet occupation in the East, civilian casualties could be huge. In addition to the 6 million Jews transported to the death camps or murdered on site, areas in which resistance or partisan activity was strongest suffered greatly. There were 3.4 million Poles, well over a million Yugoslav citizens, and about 7 million unarmed persons within the borders of the Soviet Union, who died or were killed.

Fighting in the West and the Mediterranean was smaller in scale and often less savage, as were occupation policies. But they still yielded significant losses, and – as on the Eastern Front – the experience of battle was often no less awful than on the Western Front in the First World War. Approximately half a million German servicemen died, along with approximately 350,000 British, Commonwealth, and Empire troops, and 270,000 Italian, 205,000 French, 130,000 American, 16,000 Greek, and 12,000 Dutch military personnel. As elsewhere, civilian losses were highest in occupied regions where active resistance was encountered and in fought-over regions,

Map 7. Europe 1939

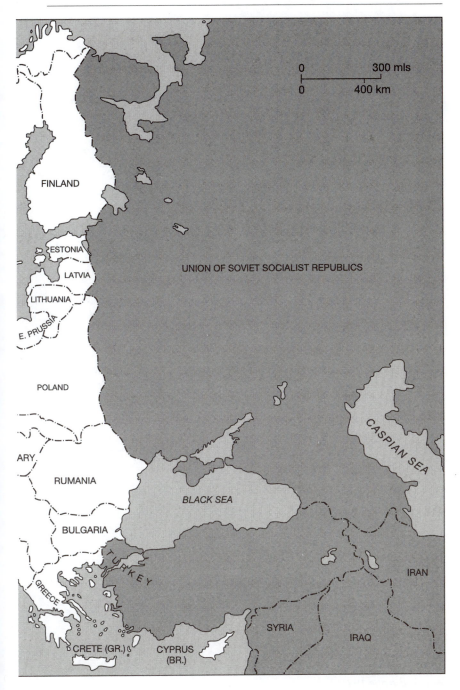

FINLAND

ESTONIA

LATVIA

LITHUANIA

E. PRUSSIA

POLAND

ARY.

RUMANIA

BULGARIA

GREECE

T U R K E Y

CRETE (GR.)

CYPRUS
(BR.)

SYRIA

IRAQ

IRAN

UNION OF SOVIET SOCIALIST REPUBLICS

BLACK SEA

CASPIAN SEA

0   300 mls

0   400 km

Map 8. Europe 1945

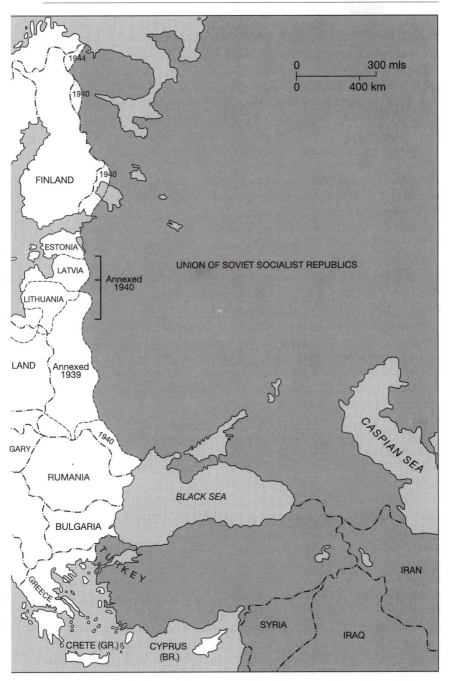

1944

1940

FINLAND

1940

ESTONIA

LATVIA

Annexed
1940

LITHUANIA

UNION OF SOVIET SOCIALIST REPUBLICS

LAND

Annexed
1939

1940

GARY

RUMANIA

BLACK SEA

CASPIAN SEA

BULGARIA

TURKEY

IRAN

GREECE

SYRIA

IRAQ

CRETE (GR.)

CYPRUS
(BR.)

0   300 mls

0   400 km

so that while Britain suffered only 95,000 civilian deaths, 132,000 Dutch, 108,000 French, and 84,000 Italian civilians died as a result of reprisals and starvation as well as the effects of both Allied and Axis military operations.

The physical destruction was also very great. Strategic bombing had caused immense damage in some British and most German cities, while in the East practically every town and city from the Vistula to the Volga had been bombed, shelled, fought over and generally laid waste. Lack of fuel and equipment meant that across the Continent transportation and communication networks were either completely lacking or minimal and in a state of grave disrepair. Agricultural production was gravely weakened, and to top things off Europe was rapidly dividing into two hostile camps.

Even as the Third Reich was going down to defeat, ideological incompatibility and contrasting visions of the postwar world were causing serious political divisions within the Grand Alliance. Joint action to win the war in Europe was one thing; co-operation in determining the shape of postwar Europe quite another.

As the war drew to a close, relations between Britain and the United States were not without friction. Anglo-American relations, however, were a study in perfect harmony compared with the growing rift between the Western Allies and the Soviet Union that would divide Europe into two hostile spheres for almost half a century. From 1941 through to 1943 the size and timing of a Second Front had been the chief bone of contention between East and West. In 1944, however, in the wake of the Normandy landings and the destruction of Army Group Centre, contrasting visions for the future of Central Europe came to the fore. In theory all three powers believed in the principles of freedom embodied in the Atlantic Charter. In practice, however, views diverged quite radically.

To Roosevelt and his successor, Harry Truman (Roosevelt having died in April 1945), those paragraphs dealing with democracy and freedom were to be taken literally, meaning free elections based on universal suffrage everywhere. Churchill was less doctrinaire. While sentimentally inclining toward the governments in exile based in London he was prepared to recognize balance-of-power realities: meaning by late 1944 the presence of the Red Army in much of Eastern Europe. For Stalin the Atlantic Charter was mere window dressing for the benefit of Britain and America, allies whose opinion was of declining importance as the Red Army surged westward. Future security for the Soviet Union in the West demanded friendly border states, meaning in practice either pliable neutrals or, more commonly, communist satellites installed by force, irrespective of local wishes. The incompatibility of these visions created frictions in which the end of the Second World War became the foundation of the Cold War.

The future of Poland was perhaps the most immediately contentious question in 1944. Relations between Moscow and the Polish government in exile based in London had always been strained. The Poles were acutely conscious of the Soviet attack of 1939 and resented pressure from Moscow via London to agree to allow the Soviet-Polish border to be moved westward once the war had been won. Stalin, knowing that German-occupied Poland had served as the central jumping-off point for Operation Barbarossa, and intensely suspicious of a Polish ruling class that had sought to expand Poland's borders at Russian expense in 1920, wanted a Poland firmly under Soviet control. By the latter part of the war, with the Red Army on the offensive, the potential for Moscow to impose its will became a reality.

Barely veiled hints by the London Poles that they considered the Soviet Union responsible for the Katyn Forest affair* (arising from the well-publicized German discovery of mass graves containing thousands of Polish officers in the former Soviet occupation zone in Poland in the spring of 1943) provided the excuse for Stalin to break off relations in April 1943 and then, in July 1944, as the Red Army stormed into Poland, to recognize formally a puppet communist movement (the Lublin Poles*). A desperate effort to assert a modicum of real sovereignty through a rising in Warsaw by the underground Polish Home Army (loyal to the London regime) in August 1944 collapsed as a result of Soviet reluctance to advance or offer aid, thus allowing time for the Germans to crush a movement which might have delayed the total subordination of Poland to Soviet aims.

Faced with increasingly naked displays of Soviet power, Churchill sought to salvage the situation in October 1944 by throwing aside principle and attempting to forge an old-fashioned balance-of-power agreement with Stalin in Moscow. In essence, Churchill recognized Soviet dominance in Eastern Europe while Stalin recognized Western dominance in Greece (where the local communists were engaged in a war with British-supported Greek forces). Churchill hoped that the recognition of a Soviet sphere of influence would allow Stalin to tolerate something other than a full-blown communist satellite.

Such an outcome, as the London Poles recognized, was highly unlikely now that Poland was being occupied by the Red Army, enabling Stalin to impose his will irrespective of Western wishes. Despite great pressure from Churchill, the London Poles refused to accept the idea of a coalition government with puppet communists, and in January

1945 the Lublin Poles were recognized as the legitimate and sole provisional government of Poland by Moscow.

Public opinion in the West could accept the incorporation of the Baltic States into the USSR, and even satellite status for much of the Balkans; but Poland was another kettle of fish. The British had gone to war to protect Poland in 1939; and Churchill, despite his agreement with Stalin, did not want to see Polish sovereignty entirely extinguished. The Americans were just as sympathetic and even more determined to see a democratic regime created in Warsaw. Unfortunately it was the Soviets who held all the cards.

At the meeting of the Big Three at Yalta* in February 1945, Roosevelt, Churchill and Stalin agreed that Poland should be moved westward, the territory lost to the Soviet Union being made up for by lands taken from Germany. With the Red Army on site the best that could be done in the way of fostering democracy was a verbal commitment by Stalin to hold free elections and a token broadening of the Lublin government with a few non-communist Poles. The subsequent Big Three meeting at Potsdam in July 1945 (in the course of which Churchill was replaced by Clement Attlee* as the chief British representative as a result of an election) witnessed a few more verbal commitments to 'free elections' and 'democracy', but it was becoming clear that Stalin was not going to be deterred by Western protests and lack of economic aid from creating one-party satellite regimes in Warsaw and everywhere else where the Red Army was in place. Hungary, Romania, and Bulgaria were all transformed into undisguised Soviet satellites in 1946–47.

To be sure the British, and later the Americans, were equally determined to limit communist influence in western and southern Europe where their own armies had acted as liberators. Communist parties in the West, however, were not banned, and with the exception of Greece, free elections and consciousness of the need for US aid rather than force and terror served as the means of preventing a domestic communist takeover in the democracies. In the Soviet sphere, by contrast, there was a growing lack of tolerance, as indicated by the arrest of non-communist politicians and churchmen, the obviously rigged Polish elections finally staged in 1947, and most blatantly by the brutal communist *coup d'état* in Prague the following year. (An increasingly independent Tito in Yugoslavia escaped a similar fate because his partisans had seized power at the end of the war without much aid from the Red Army and hence Stalin lacked enough military and political leverage in the country to stage a successful *coup*.)

Even more problematic than Poland and southeastern Europe was the German Question. It had been agreed in early 1944 and confirmed at Yalta in January 1945 that Germany should be divided into four military occupation zones (Soviet, British, American and French). These zones, as it happened, more or less mirrored the extent of Anglo-American and Soviet military advances in the last months of the war. Beyond that, however, and agreement that surviving Nazi leaders should be held accountable for their actions (the 1946 Nuremburg trials), no consensus existed. With no single power dominant throughout the country, the potential for long-term friction was greater than elsewhere in Central Europe. By 1947, however stridently the Western Powers might protest, the future of Poland had been determined by its presence within a single sphere of influence. The future of Germany, divided between East and West, would poison relations for the rest of the decade and firmly entrench hostile attitudes.

At Potsdam and subsequently, the British and American desire to see German exports revive in order to fund food imports and help the wider European economy, repeatedly ran up against Soviet demands for high reparations (which the Western Powers thought would cripple recovery) and fears of a German revival. In 1946, reparations in kind to the East were suspended, and the British and American zones merged without Russian consent. The American financial effort to boost European recovery (the Marshall Plan) deliberately included western Germany, and in June 1948 the first steps toward an independent West German state were announced. Seeking to assert the right of the USSR to a voice in determining the fate of Germany, Stalin retaliated by blocking land routes to Berlin (under four-power control but deep in the Soviet zone) in an effort to force the Western Powers to give it up. A large-scale Anglo-American airlift effort undercut the effects of the land blockade, which was lifted in May 1949. The ending of the Berlin blockade, which had brought Europe once more to the brink of war, eased tensions somewhat, but also confirmed suspicions. By the end of the decade mutual distrust and hostility were so great that negotiating a pan-German or any other settlement had become impossible [164].

By the 1950s Europe was sharply divided between East and West, and Germany itself split into two states. On either side of what Churchill called the Iron Curtain, states were organized into hostile political, economic and military blocs dominated by the United States on the one hand and the Soviet Union on the other. The Security Council of the United Nations, set up in 1945 to perpetuate the Grand Alliance and preserve the peace, had become a forum for hostile rhetoric and posturing from which co-operative action almost never emerged. In the defeat of the Axis lay the seeds of the Cold War.

HISTORICAL DEBATES

The sheer size and complexity of the Second World War have tended to generate a host of varying interpretations on a myriad of particular episodes. The passage of time and the evolution of politics, meanwhile, as well as popular and academic culture have also tended to continually reshape the overall context of thinking about the war.

Broadly speaking, historiographical debate in the English-speaking world has tended to focus on three general themes. The first concerns those events which appear either as key military or political turning-points in the course of the fighting: often in the context of the postwar division of Europe (e.g. Allied approaches in the West, Unconditional Surrender). The second theme relates to episodes seen as particularly significant in moral terms (Allied strategic bombing and the Holocaust). The third theme involves the social impact of the war.

Within the first category, debate has tended to lean towards events in the second half of the struggle. There were, however, two episodes from the earlier part of the war of such strategic magnitude that they could not but generate debate. The first was the collapse of France in 1940, which dramatically shifted the balance of fortune in Germany's favour. The second was the failure of Operation Barbarossa the following year, which marked the beginning of the end for the tide of German conquest. Alternative outcomes in either case might have significantly altered the course of the war: in the former case in the Allies' favour, in the latter in Germany's favour.

The defeat of France within six weeks of the opening of the German offensive in the West came as a great shock and explanations were naturally sought after. The general tendency over the next forty or so years was to explain defeat at least partly in terms of structural weaknesses within French politics and society; weaknesses that in turn generated a poor military showing in 1940 [64]. More recently, however, emphasis has shifted toward doctrinal issues as the primary determinant in French defeat. A faulty approach to military operations, rather than any national malaise, is now often seen as the cause of the 1940 débâcle [58].

In comparison with the debates over events in the West, questions arising from the war in the East have been comparatively few in English-language studies (partly a matter of Anglo-American chauvinism and partly a matter of a lack of proper access to Soviet archival sources). Nevertheless, one question has been a consistent subject of scrutiny: what were the reasons for German failure to achieve another knock-out victory in Operation Barbarossa?

One explanation, popularized by Churchill shortly after the war, was that the campaign in the Balkans fatally delayed the opening of the German offensive against the Soviet Union. If Barbarossa had been launched in May 1941 the German army would have had more time to exploit its victories and reach Moscow before winter set in and immobilized the Panzer arm. More recent scholarship, however, reflected in the survey literature, has suggested that the wet spring would have delayed the opening of Barbarossa in any event and that the German thrusts were already failing before winter arrived [10, 15].

Then there is the related question of whether a fleeting opportunity to take Moscow had been wasted. Was Hitler's decision in August 1941 to divert armoured formations away from Army Group Centre and the main axis of advance fatal to the *Wehrmacht*'s chances of taking the capital (and thereby dealing the Soviet regime a mortal blow)?

In their memoirs the German generals certainly thought so, implying in light of the Cold War that such an outcome would have been preferable to Eastern Europe being reduced to a series of Soviet satellites after 1945. A fair number of English-language historians of the war, while not possessing quite the same anti-Soviet bias, have concurred in thinking that an opportunity to take Moscow was missed [10, 13, 77].

Other historians, however, regard the issue as irrelevant: a conclusion given added weight by growing knowledge of the Soviet war effort. Germany was simply not strong enough to conquer Russia even in 1941, let alone in later years [15, 74, 169].

Another long-running strategic debate, again often framed within the context of the Cold War, centres on Allied decisions concerning the relative priority accorded to the Mediterranean as against the Second Front between 1942 and 1944. At the root have been two issues: whether an opportunity to move into southeastern Europe before the Red Army got there was wasted by diversion of resources away from the Mediterranean, and, conversely, whether the war could have been shortened by concentration on establishing a Second Front in France instead of pursuing a Mediterranean strategy.

Very roughly speaking, postwar argument tended to mirror wartime divisions. American and Soviet historians, official and otherwise, highlighted the importance of the Second Front, while British historians stressed the virtues of the Mediterranean approach [5, 125, 126].

More recent scholarship, however, placing Anglo-American strategy in wider political and geopolitical context and reflected in the more recent surveys, has tended to stress the inevitability of the compromise strategy reached at the Teheran conference. Given the balance of forces available, a cross-Channel attack in 1943 would almost certainly have failed to achieved the success of Overlord in 1944. Moreover, while never possessing the potential for exploitation northward that Churchill hoped, fighting in the Mediterranean in 1942–43 was both politically expedient (doing something while forces for the cross-Channel attack were built up) and militarily useful (tying down German forces and forcing Hitler to worry about further landings on the Southern Front) [10, 15].

A concurrent and linked debate on Allied strategy concerned the policy of Unconditional Surrender and the outcome of the Yalta conference. To some observers, Unconditional Surrender only made the Germans fight harder and shut the door on the possibility of a negotiated surrender by non-Nazi Germans that might have occurred before the Red Army had overrun all of Eastern Europe. Similarly, Allied concessions made to Stalin at the Yalta conference over the political future of Eastern Europe in return for promises to join the war against Japan sealed the region's postwar fate [13]. To historians of more recent vintage, however, this view appears ahistorical. Unconditional Surrender was a logical outgrowth of total war, contributed to Allied unity, and did little to alter the outcome of the war and the shape of postwar Europe. As for Yalta, Stalin got nothing there that he was not able to achieve in Eastern Europe through the presence of the Red Army [16].

The final major Anglo-American debate concerning Allied strategy, once again linked with the onset of the Cold War, relates to Allied strategy after the Normandy breakout. Some British historians asserted, or implied, that Eisenhower squandered a chance at final victory in late 1944 – and thus, presumably, a chance at perhaps occupying Berlin before the Russians arrived – by opting for a broad-front offensive against Germany rather than a more concentrated, dagger-like thrust [8, 33].

Eisenhower himself in his memoirs and later his principal biographer and others countered that political considerations and logistics – the latter point and Monty's failure to address it are seen as vitally important in the most recent general studies – ruled out a narrow-thrust approach. The Americans would not stand for a single British-led advance, while even the British staff at SHAEF (Supreme Headquarters Allied Expeditionary Forces) were sceptical that Montgomery could achieve his goals given the precarious state of Allied logistics at this time – this second issue being regarded as definitive in some of the more recent British and American surveys [10, 27, 169]. The debate, however, rumbles on [162].

Not all major debates about wartime events have had a Cold War subtext. There also have been moral questions to consider, particularly in relation to justifications for the Allied strategic bombing campaign and explanations for the Final Solution.

The debate over strategic bombing has centred on two intertwined issues: whether it was effective and whether it was morally justified. Predictably, the postwar studies conducted by the air forces – which continue to attract some support – concluded that bombing had done much to undermine the German war machine [141]. Many contemporary historians, however, have indicated the high costs and real limits to Allied achievement until 1944–45 and the ways in which resources devoted to the campaign might have been used to better effect in, say, helping win the Battle of the Atlantic in 1942–43 [137, 145].

There are, in addition, those who argue that strategic bombing was not only ineffective but also immoral, in that it was aimed, directly or indirectly, at noncombatants. Debate continues as to whether or not new navigation aids introduced in the course of the war made more precise night bombing feasible. But most historians now agree that, even if the aim of breaking civilian morale through area bombing at night in order to shorten the war was ethical, it was pursued by RAF Bomber Command under Harris well beyond the point where it was evident that it was not going to work [133].

A much sharper division divides observers concerning the morality of the USAAF daylight strategic bombing campaign. Much depends here on whether one concludes that Spaatz and others ignored, or continued to adhere to, the stated goal of precision bombing when using imprecise radar rather than visual targeting equipment in the winter of 1944–45. There is evidence to suggest that precision bombing was being discarded in practice if not in theory [143]. There is also evidence supporting the idea that the American bomber barons were doing their best to play by the rules under difficult circumstances [132].

The horrors of indiscriminate bombing, however, pale beside the enormity of the Holocaust. Few other episodes have generated as much historical scrutiny. Much – though by no means all – is now known about what happened. More problematic is the question of when and why. Was the Final Solution something that inevitably arose from Hitler's own long-term ideological obsessions [110]? Or was it something much more specific to wartime conditions arrived at somewhat haphazardly through a complex bureaucratic decision-making process within the Nazi hierarchy rather than Hitler alone [108, 115]? And just how culpable were ordinary Germans? Were they pawns or agents [109, 112]?

There is also the knotty question of whether the Allies could have limited the death toll by bombing the railways leading to the extermination camps. Some observers argue that the Allies were wilfully negligent in this and other respects when it came to the Holocaust [118]. Others suggest that, as with the strategic bombing campaign in general, there were both technical limitations and the resilience of the German industrial complex to consider: would the machinery of destruction have proved any easier to stop than the machinery of production? The Allies, according to this counterargument, were right to concentrate on winning the war as a means of halting the slaughter [116].

The third major area of historical debate centres on the vexed question of whether or not the socio-economic upheaval of the war years produced any long-term socio-political change in the Allied camp. Here too established views have been challenged.

The initial assumption was that wartime conditions had fostered a mildly collectivist and generally positive semi-consensus within societies that in turn helped to further the development of postwar state interventionism. It was also thought that the war greatly increased economic and other opportunities for women. More recently, however, the nature of the 'Good War' social experience, as well as its impact on postwar society, have been challenged. Particularly with regard to Britain and America, wartime fissures along lines of class, race (USA), gender and politics have all been highlighted, raising questions as to the nature and impact of the wartime experience.

Did the war help create an enduring socio-political consensus [78, 82, 96]? Or did the wartime experience mask longer-term continuities and divisions in – for instance – British society and politics [81, 88]? Did the enlistment of women into the industrial workforce herald a significant long-term expansion of women's socio-economic opportunities [85]? Or did deep-rooted cultural assumptions among both men and women tend to stress a return to the *status quo* after 1945 [79, 98]?

Debates about particular themes aside, the most central historical question concerning the Second World War remains the causes and nature of victory and defeat. Why, then, did the Axis powers lose and the Allies win in Europe?

WINNING AND LOSING

Economic factors would seem to be one overarching answer. Before the upheaval of the summer of 1940 the two sides had been more or less evenly matched in terms of relative war potential. The active participation of Fascist Italy and the elimination of France, a leading member of the initial Allied coalition (as well as its subsequent partial incorporation into the Axis diplomatic and war production sphere), altered the balance of power heavily in favour of Nazi Germany. The entry into the war of the USA the following year, however, coupled with the survival of the USSR, created a situation in which Hitler and his junior partners were facing enemies whose combined industrial war potential in terms of exploitable human and material resources was much greater than that of the Reich and conquered Europe. Even allowing for the huge destruction and dislocation caused in the Soviet Union in 1941–42, and the ongoing need by the USA to fight a war in the Pacific as well as Europe, the gulf in economic power appears wide enough to have been a decisive factor. The human and material resources with which to produce and man the machines of total war – the ships, aircraft, tanks, guns, and so forth – were indeed available in larger quantities on the Allied side than on the Axis from 1942 onward. Not surprisingly, therefore, there emerged a growing disparity in the size of the combined armed forces and, above all, in the number of available war machines. By 1943, for example, overall Allied armaments production was three times greater than that of the Axis powers (including Japan).

Did the Allies thus win simply because of greater economic potential? Though relative human and material resources such as fossil fuels, arable land and iron ore deposits were a prerequisite, they do not in and of themselves explain Axis defeat. Ultimately of more significance than the relative resource base was the willingness and ability to exploit it effectively, both in terms of war production and actual war fighting [173].

In terms of maximizing war production, Fascist Italy never managed to achieve much success in harnessing its limited resources effectively. Within the Third Reich, however, the streamlining and rationalizing efforts of armaments minister Speer were spectacularly successful. Between 1941 and 1944, for instance, the number of combat aircraft produced in Germany annually increased more than threefold to reach a peak of 39,807. The problem was that the Allies were even more successful in effectively organizing war production. Structural weaknesses in the British industrial sector may have limited increases in production, yet from the start the British war economy was well managed and output remained quite high from 1940 through to 1945 (over 26,000 combat aircraft both in 1943 and 1944, for instance). The Soviet Union, with a longer history of centrally directed economic planning in labour allocation and the development of heavy industry, managed to recover from the disasters of 1941–42 and go on to recreate a war economy of massive proportions. By 1944 over 40,000 rugged combat aircraft were emerging from the factories. Above all, and with far less overt coercive effort, the United States was able to harness effectively its huge latent war potential. By 1943 aircraft production in the USA – some of which went to Britain and the USSR through Lend-Lease – had reached an annual total of nearly 87,000; more than enough to give the Allies an overall productive advantage of 3.5 to 1 over the Axis.

The Allies, in short, proved able to capitalize on their latent economic advantage, in all cases creating and modifying bureaucratic mechanisms – ministries, commissariats, boards – with which to exploit effectively available resources. Furthermore, ideological considerations (with respect to the roles of non-Aryan races and women), combined with political considerations (Hitler's arbitrary creation of competing bureaucracies with overlapping spheres of authority in order to maintain his position as the ultimate arbiter), meant that the Third Reich, even in the Speer years, never achieved its full productive potential.

Resources and their effective exploitation, however, cannot by themselves explain why one side won and the other lost. National morale, the will to make great material sacrifices and tenaciously go on fighting was also of great significance. Victory and limited calls for sacrifice sustained German morale in the early years of the war. Later on effective state propaganda (playing on fears of what would happen to Germany in defeat [*Doc. 11*]) buttressed faith in the Führer and, along with ferocious disciplinary measures [*Doc. 22*], kept Germans working and fighting hard up to 1944–45 [171].

Commitment to making all necessary sacrifices for victory among Italians was much less evident, as both battlefield performance and the events of 1943 demonstrated. Yet German tenaciousness, combined with greater tactical skill in land warfare, could conceivably have negated the Allied edge in material if the peoples of the Allied states themselves had not proven willing to make the necessary sacrifices. As it happened, however, for the most part they did prove willing. British morale was occasionally shaken by battlefield reverses and the effects of air bombardment. Nevertheless, through adaptation and the maintenance of democratic forms, whereby a degree of dissent and criticism through the press and parliament was tolerated (albeit sometimes grudgingly) by the government and other authorities, British civilians and servicemen alike proved willing to meet Churchill's call for 'blood, sweat and tears' [*Doc. 4*] in order to defeat Nazi Germany. Even in the darkest days of 1940–41 the British did not, as Hitler had expected, throw in the towel [170].

Hitler was also wrong in expressing the view that Americans lacked the moral fibre to withstand heavy losses in battle. The skill and tenacity of the *Wehrmacht* often came as a shock to American soldiers new to battle. But, like their British counterparts, American fighting men adapted, relying on firepower to make up for lack of tactical finesse and never suffering a general loss of will to fight [168, 169, 174].

Within the Soviet Union in 1941–42, to be sure, the oppressive nature of the communist regime coupled with the massive scale of German victories made some soldiers and civilians, especially among the non-Russian peoples, unwilling to sacrifice everything for the cause. The sheer barbarity of German occupation policies, however, made Stalin seem the lesser of two evils: especially once calls for sacrifice were couched in terms of traditional patriotism rather than communism. Coupled with a coercive state apparatus that matched that of Nazi Germany, this meant that Soviet people, both soldiers and civilians, proved capable of making almost superhuman sacrifices rather than give up [167].

Germany did not, therefore, have a monopoly in maintaining the will to win. This in turn meant that greater Allied resources and their effective management ultimately took their toll [172].

What was more, Axis defeat was hastened by the disparity in the quality of strategic decision making. Here the Allies generated a tremendous advantage.

Mechanisms for effective joint planning by the European Axis powers never emerged, and until Italy came to rely on German power to rescue it from the consequences of independent action in 1941 and thereafter both Mussolini and Hitler pursued largely independent strategies that were in some respects at cross purposes. Subsequently, to be sure, greater coherence was achieved through Germany assuming a leading role in the Mediterranean theatre; but, as the efforts to conclude a separate peace in 1943 indicate, many leading figures in Rome had come to recognize that this coherence was simply the result of Italian interests being increasingly subordinated to German interests. A similar situation existed with respect to the smaller and even weaker German satellites in southeastern Europe.

Given the predominance of German power on the Axis side this state of affairs might not have affected the course of the war if strategic decision making within the Third Reich had been based on rational calculation and professional appreciation. Instead, it was increasingly based on the will of Hitler and Hitler alone, a dictator whose grasp of strategy was undermined by unfounded *a priori* assumptions concerning the nature of Germany's foes, distrust of professional advice (something also true of Mussolini), and above all a pathological desire to act offensively rather than accept a defensive posture. Especially in the later years of the war, Hitler's decisions on all fronts hastened the hour of German defeat by repeatedly placing German forces in untenable positions.

On the Anglo-American side, conversely, strategy was in general well thought out via bureaucratic mechanisms such as the combined Chiefs of Staff and by civilian heads of state who, at root, understood the need to listen to professional advice and compromise with major allies. There was plenty of friction, but also plenty of rational thinking. Allied strategic consultation and co-operation with the Soviet Union was much more limited and fraught with greater suspicion; but it did nevertheless exist. Stalin, moreover, unlike Hitler, learned over time to place some trust in the professional judgement of Stavka and senior commanders, thereby increasing the effectiveness of Soviet military operations from the latter part of 1942 onward.

Human factors, in short, are as significant as material factors in explaining the outcome of the war. The relative importance of various factors within these two overall categories, along with particular episodes and subjects, continue to be subject to debate.

PART FOUR: DOCUMENTS

DOCUMENT 1   **BRITAIN GOES TO WAR**

On 3 September 1939, three days into the German invasion of Poland, Prime Minister Neville Chamberlain announced to the House of Commons the circumstances surrounding the British government's decision to declare war on the Third Reich.

When I spoke last night to the House I could not but be aware that in some parts of the House there were doubts and some bewilderment as to whether there had been any weakening, hesitation or vacillation on the part of His Majesty's Government ... . The statement which I have to make this morning will show that there were no grounds for doubt. We were in consultation all day yesterday with the French Government and we felt that the intensified action which the Germans were taking against Poland allowed no delay in making our own position clear. Accordingly, we decided to send to our own Ambassador in Berlin instructions which he was to hand at nine o'clock this morning to the German Foreign Secretary and which read as follows:

'Sir,
In the communication which I had the honour to make to you on 1 September, I informed you, on the instructions of His Majesty's Principal Secretary of State for Foreign Affairs, that unless the German Government were prepared to give His Majesty's Government in the United Kingdom satisfactory assurances that the German Government had suspended all aggressive action against Poland and were prepared promptly to withdraw their forces from Polish territory, His Majesty's Government in the United Kingdom would, without hesitation, fulfil their obligations to Poland.
    Although this communication was made more than 24 hours ago, no reply has been received, but German attacks upon Poland have been continued and intensified. I have, accordingly, the honour to inform you that unless no later than 11 a.m., British Summer Time, to-day, September 3rd, satisfactory assurances to the above effect have been given by the German Government and have reached His Majesty's Gov-

ernment in London, a state of war will exist between the two countries as from that hour.'

That was the final Note. No such undertaking was received by the time stipulated, and, consequently, this country is at war with Germany.

House of Commons Debates, 5th Series, Vol. 351, cols 291–2.

DOCUMENT 2   **THE MOOD IN BERLIN**

William Shirer, an American journalist who witnessed the Third Reich at first hand in Berlin as a correspondent in the 1930s, was struck by the contrast between the mood on the outbreak of war in 1914 and the mood in 1939.

In 1914, I believe, the excitement in Berlin on the first day of the World War was tremendous. Today, no excitement, no hurrahs, no cheering, no throwing of flowers, no war fever, no hysteria. There is not even any hate for the French and British – despite Hitler's various proclamations to the people, the party, the East Army, the West Army, accusing the 'English warmongers and capitalistic Jews' of starting this war. When I passed the French and British embassies this afternoon [3 Sep. 1939], the sidewalk in front of each of them was deserted.

W. L. Shirer, *Berlin Diary: The Journal of a Foreign Correspondent, 1934–1941*, Knopf, New York, 1941, p. 201.

DOCUMENT 3   **BLITZKRIEG 1940**

In his memoirs General Erich von Manstein reproduced the principles that would serve as the basis of the successful Blitzkrieg *campaign against France in May–June 1940.*

1. The *aim of the offensive* must be to *achieve decisive results on land*. The political and military stakes are too high for the limited objectives defined in the present Operation Order, i.e. defeat of the largest possible elements of the enemy in Belgium and occupation of parts of the Channel coast. Final victory on land must be the goal.
The operations must therefore be directed towards winning a final decision in France and destroying France's resistance.
2. This ... requires that the main point of effort be placed unequivocally on the southern wing from the start, i.e. with Army Group A ...
If the main effort is transferred to Army Group A in the south, the task of which is to drive through southern Belgium and over the Meuse in the direction

of the *lower Somme*, the strong enemy forces expected in northern Belgium must, if thrown back by Army Group B in frontal attack, be cut off and destroyed. This will be possible only if Army Group A drives swiftly through to the lower Somme. That must be the first phase of the campaign. The second will be the envelopment of the whole French Army with a powerful right hook.

3. To fulfil this task, Army Group A must consist of *three armies* ...

It is essential that the *Luftwaffe* smash the French troop concentrations at an early date ... .

E. von Manstein, *Lost Victories*, Henry Regnery, Chicago, 1958, pp. 121–2.

DOCUMENT 4   CHURCHILL'S FINEST HOUR

On 13 May 1940, three days after becoming Prime Minister of Great Britain, Winston Churchill explained to the House of Commons his war policy as the Germans swept westward.

On Friday evening last I received His Majesty's Commission to form a new Administration. It was the evident wish and will of Parliament and the nation that this should be conceived on the broadest possible basis and that it should include all parties... .

I hope that any of my friends and colleagues, or former colleagues, who are affected by the political reconstruction, will make allowance, all allowance, for any lack of ceremony with which it has been necessary to act. I would say to the House, as I said to those who have joined this Government: 'I have nothing to offer but blood, toil, tears and sweat.'

We have before us an ordeal of the most grievous kind. We have before us many, many long months of struggle and of suffering. You may ask, what is our policy? I can say: It is to wage war, by sea, land and air, with all our might and with all the strength that God can give us; to wage war against a monstrous tyranny, never surpassed in the dark, lamentable catalogue of human crime. That is our policy. You ask, what is our aim? I can answer in one word: It is victory, victory at all costs, victory in spite of all terror, victory, however long and hard the road may be; for without victory, there is no survival. Let that be realised; no survival for the British Empire, no survival for all the British Empire has stood for, no survival for the urge and impulse of the ages that mankind will move forward towards its goal. But I take up my task with buoyancy and hope. I feel sure that our cause will not be suffered to fail among men. At this time I feel entitled to claim the aid of all, and I say, 'Come then, let us go forward together with our united strength.'

R. Rhodes James (ed.), *Winston S. Churchill, His Complete Speeches 1897–1963: Vol. VI, 1935–1942*, Chelsea House, London, 1974, pp. 6219–6220.

DOCUMENT 5   DE GAULLE AND RESISTANCE

Stranded in Britain while acting as Reynaud's deputy minster of defence at the time of the final French collapse in June 1940, General Charles de Gaulle refused to accept defeat. On 19 June, only days before a Franco-German armistice was signed by representatives of the Pétain regime, he called on the French to continue fighting in a radio broadcast from London.

Faced by the bewilderment of my countrymen, by the disintegration of a Government in thrall to the enemy, by the fact that the institutions of my country are incapable of functioning, I, General de Gaulle, a French soldier and military leader, realise that I now speak for France.

In the name of France, I make the following solemn declaration:

It is the bounden duty of all Frenchmen who still bear arms to continue the struggle. For them to lay down their arms ... would be a crime against our country.

...

Soldiers of France, wherever you may be, arise!

C. de Gaulle, *War Memoirs, Volume One: The Call to Honour, 1940–1942, Documents*, Collins, London, 1955, p. 13.

DOCUMENT 6   STALIN AND BARBAROSSA

The initial success of the German assault on the USSR in June 1941 was due in part to Stalin's refusal to act on intelligence reports of an imminent attack. Nikita Khrushchev, his successor, explained why in his memoirs.

When the enemy first launched the invasion, we received orders from Moscow not to shoot back. Our leaders issued this strange command because they thought that possibly the artillery fire was a provocation on the part of some German field commander acting independently of Hitler. In other words, Stalin was so afraid of war that even when the Germans tried to take us by surprise and wipe out our resistance, Stalin convinced himself that Hitler would keep his word and wouldn't really attack us.

N. S. Khrushchev, *Khrushchev Remembers*, S. Talbot, trans., Little Brown, Boston, 1970, pp. 167–8.

DOCUMENT 7   ITALO-GERMAN RELATIONS

As the following January 1942 extract from the diary of Mussolini's Foreign Minister, Count Ciano, suggests, most Germans barely hid their contempt for their Italian allies, treating them little differently than the peoples of Occupied Europe.

Again Mussolini complains of the behaviour of the Germans in Italy. He has before him the transcript of a telephone call by one of Kesselring's aides, who, speaking with Berlin, called us 'macaroni' and hoped that Italy, too, would become an occupied country. The Duce is keeping a dossier of all this, which 'is to be used when the moment comes.' In the meantime, he reacts strongly against the request ... to have still more Italian workingmen sent to Germany. They would like to raise the number from two hundred thousand to three hundred and twenty-five thousand. It is too much. Moreover, it is impossible because, aside from other considerations, our own labour supply is running short and we shall soon have to call new classes to the colours.

The Ciano Diaries, 1939–1943: The Complete, Unabridged Diaries of Count Galeazzo Ciano, Italian Minister for Foreign Affairs, 1936–1943, H. Gibson (ed), Garden City, New York, 1947, pp. 493–4.

DOCUMENT 8   STALINGRAD DIARY

The following extracts from a German soldier's diary, picked up after the German surrender, graphically indicate the increasingly desperate situation of the German 6th Army in its final months of existence.

November 29. We are encircled. It was announced this morning that the Führer had said: 'The army can trust me to do everything necessary to ensure supplies and rapidly break the [Soviet] encirclement.'
December 3. We are on hunger rations and waiting for the rescue that the Führer promised.

I send letters home, but there is no reply.

December 7. Rations have been cut to such an extent that the soldiers are suffering terribly from hunger; they are issuing one loaf of stale bread for five men.
December 11. Three questions are obsessing every soldier and officer: When will the Russians stop firing and let us sleep in peace, if only for one night? How and with what are we going to fill our empty stomachs, which, apart from $3\frac{1}{2}$ – 7 ozs of bread, receive virtually nothing at all? And when will Hitler take any decisive steps to free our armies from encirclement?

December 14. Everybody is wracked with hunger. Frozen potatoes are the best meal, but to get them out of the ice-covered ground under fire from Russian bullets is not so easy.

December 18. The officers today told the soldiers to be prepared for action. General Manstein is approaching Stalingrad from the south with strong forces. This news brought hope to the soldiers' hearts. God, let it be!

December 21. We are waiting for the order, but for some reason or other it has been a long time coming. Can it be that it is not true about Manstein? This is worse than any torture.

December 23. Still no orders. It was all a bluff with Manstein. Or has he been defeated at the approaches to Stalingrad?

December 25. The Russian radio has announced the defeat of Manstein. Ahead of us is either death or captivity.

December 26. The horses have already been eaten. I would eat a cat; they say its meat is also tasty. The soldiers look like corpses or lunatics, looking for something to put in their mouths. They no longer take cover from Russian shells; they haven't the strength to walk, run away and hide. A curse on this war!

Diary of a German soldier, in V. Chuikov, *The Battle for Stalingrad*, Grafton Books, New York, pp. 253–4.

DOCUMENT 9   **THE RED ARMY**

As Field-Marshal Ewald von Kleist indicated in a postwar interview, the combination of the ordinary soldier's toughness and Stavka's growing professionalism made the Red Army a formidable foe for the Wehrmacht.

The men were first-rate *fighters* from the start, and we owed our success simply to superior training. They became first-rate *soldiers* with experience. They fought most toughly, had amazing endurance, and could carry on without most of the things which other armies regarded as necessities. The Staff was quick to learn and soon became highly efficient.

Von Kleist quoted in B. H. Liddell Hart, *The Other Side of the Hill*, Cassell, London, 1951, p. 329.

DOCUMENT 10   **HIMMLER ON RACE**

In a speech to SS generals delivered in October 1943, SS-chief Heinrich Himmler emphasized the logical consequences of Nazi race theory.

One basic principle must be the absolute rule for the SS man: we must be honest, decent, loyal, and comradely to members of our own blood and to nobody else. What happens to a Russian, to a Czech does not interest me in the slightest. What the nations can offer in the way of good blood of our type, we will take, if necessary by kidnapping their children and raising them here with us. Whether nations live in prosperity or starve to death like cattle interests me only in so far as we need them as slaves for our Kultur; otherwise, it is of no interest to me. Whether 10,000 Russian females fall down from exhaustion while digging an anti-tank ditch interests me only in so far as the anti-tank ditch for Germany is finished. We shall never be rough and heartless when it is not necessary, that is clear. We Germans, who are the only people in the world to have a decent attitude towards animals, will also assume a decent attitude towards these human animals. But it is a crime against our own blood to worry about them and give them ideals, thus causing our sons and grandsons to have a more difficult time with them. When somebody comes to me and says, 'I cannot dig this anti-tank ditch with women and children, it is inhuman, for it would kill them,' then I would have to say, 'You are a murderer of your own blood because if the anti-tank ditch is not dug, German soldiers will die, and they are the sons of German mothers. They are our own blood.' That is what I want to instill into the SS ... . Our concern, our duty is our people and our blood. It is for them that we must provide and plan, work and fight, nothing else. We can be indifferent to everything else. I wish the SS to adopt this attitude to the problem of all foreign, non-German peoples, especially Russians.

Doc. 1919-PS, *Nazi Conspiracy and Aggression, Vol. IV*, USGPO, Washington, DC, 1946.

DOCUMENT 11   GOEBBELS AND TERROR PROPAGANDA

Foreigners put to work in the German economy had a unique opportunity to observe the behaviour and attitudes of ordinary Germans at close hand. Edward Ward, a British prisoner, later recorded his impressions of the effectiveness of Nazi propaganda concerning the Red Menace.

I had talked to hundreds of them ... they [the German people in 1944] were obsessed with fear of the Bolshevist bogey.

In this at least Doctor Goebbels' propaganda had hit the mark. The radio blared forth about the terrors of Bolshevism, the newspapers were full of atrocity stories from East Prussia, every railway station, every locomotive had a great sign painted on it, 'SIEG ODER BOLSCHEWISMUS – Victory or Bolshevism' – and no matter what else the Germans disbelieved of their own propaganda, the Bolshevist bogey sank home. They were genuinely terrified of the Russians. And Goebbels played on this fear for all he was worth. It was the real driving force of his amazing propaganda machine. I marvelled at Goebbels' skill every time I listened to his weekly Friday talks on the radio ... . every week he contrived to build something out of nothing.

E. Ward, *Give Me Air*, John Lane: London, 1946, p. 140. (Ward was a captured British journalist.)

DOCUMENT 12   UNCONDITIONAL SURRENDER

One of the more controversial of Allied policies, first enunciated by President Roosevelt after the Casablanca conference in January 1943, was Unconditional Surrender. Churchill later sought to explain its meaning in the House of Commons.

The term 'unconditional surrender' does not mean that the German people will be enslaved or destroyed. It means however that the Allies will not be bound to them at the moment of surrender by any pact or obligation. There will be, for instance, no question of the Atlantic Charter applying to Germany as a matter of right and barring territorial transferences or adjustments in enemy countries.

   ... Unconditional surrender means that the victors will have a free hand. It does not mean that they are entitled to behave in a barbarous manner, nor that they wish to blot out Germany from among the nations of Europe. If we are bound, we are bound by our own consciences to civilisation. We are not to be bound to the Germans as the result of a bargain struck. That is the meaning of 'unconditional surrender.'

Churchill's address to the House of Commons, 22 February 1943. W. S. Churchill, *The Second World War, Vol. 4: The Hinge of Fate*, Houghton Mifflin, Boston, 1950, pp. 334–5.

DOCUMENT 13   WORKERS' ATTITUDES IN WARTIME BRITAIN

The following extract from a study of a war production factory in England, carried out in 1942, indicates the limits of personal commitment to the war effort.

The basic trouble with this factory (and with many others too) is one which lies quite outside the scope of miscellaneous tinkering with conditions and regulations. It lies at the very roots of this country's attitude to its wartime life. The war is regarded (by many young working girls) with mainly negative emotions. The cardinal virtue is the negative one of endurance; endurance of danger; endurance of a distasteful job; endurance of shortages. And because the war has been put across with complete success as something to be endured (and after twenty years of anti-war emotion this was almost the only way in which it could be put across), not as something to be plunged into with zest and enthusiasm, this attitude of endurance is the one which people primarily bring to all the changes in their personal lives which the war has caused. They regard their new lives, not as an exciting adventure, full of new personal and social possibilities, but as something to be put up with until at last the peace life can be taken up again. The ambition that keeps [directed working] girls going is not the hope of achieving something in the new life, but the hope that the peace will return soon. So far from wanting to make good under present conditions, the all-absorbing hope is that present conditions and all appertaining to them will, as soon as possible, have vanished, never to be thought of again.

Mass-Observation, *War Factory: A Report*, Gollancz, London, 1943, pp. 121–2.

DOCUMENT 14   **ALLIED PRODUCTION OPERATIONS COMPARED**

British industry's sometimes rather antiquated approach to production-line efficiency is highlighted in the following extract from a British mission report written after a visit to US plants.

The various [aircraft] production operations are broken down into stages and planned more elaborately in America than in this country [Britain]. Much time and effort is put into pre-preparation work of scheduling, process planning, machine loading, labour loading and shop layout and this is carried out in greater detail in America than is customary in many of our factories. This is considered to be an essential part of obtaining efficient production. Time study is extensively used as a means of obtaining adequate data for this work.

British mission report on USA visit, June 1943, quoted in C. Barnett [81], p. 153.

DOCUMENT 15   **SPEER ON ALLIED BOMBING**

As Armaments Minister during the worst of the Allied air assault on Germany, Albert Speer was in a uniquely strong position to judge the effectiveness of the combined bombing campaign. Here is what he had to say in his memoirs.

Neither did the bombing and the hardships that resulted from them weaken the morale of the populace. On the contrary, from my visits to armaments plants and my contacts with the man in the street I carried away the impression of growing toughness. It may well be that the estimated loss of nine per cent of our production capacity was amply balanced by our increased effort.

Our heaviest expense was in fact the elaborate defensive measures. In the Reich and in the western theatres of war the barrels of ten thousand anti-aircraft guns were pointed towards the sky. The same guns could have been employed in Russia against tanks and other ground targets. Had it not been for this new front, the air front over Germany, our defensive strength against tanks would have been about doubled, as far as equipment was concerned. Moreover, the anti-aircraft force tied down hundreds of thousands of young soldiers. A third of the optical industry was busy producing gunsights for the flak batteries. About half of the electronics industry was engaged in producing radar and communications networks for defence against bombing. Simply because of this, in spite of the high level of the German electronics and optical industries, the supply of our frontline troops with modern equipment remained far behind that of the Western armies.

A. Speer [25], pp. 278–9.

DOCUMENT 16   **UNDER THE BOMBS**

German civilian morale did not break as a result of RAF bombing, but the experience was not one that anybody wished to repeat. The following recollection by a Berlin typist of a November 1943 raid on the capital illustrates the terror and destruction that the bombs could create.

We had to go down to the cellar ... .We put on our warm clothes and took our small air-raid suitcase and a book to read ... . I remember all this clearly because those were the last memories of my home. We all had our own regular seats in the shelter. We sat there, with our little cases and our hot coffee or tea, because there was no heating in the shelter. It is difficult to describe one's feelings – somewhere between anxiety and hope. Sometimes someone would try and cheer things up with a little joke, specially for the children, but really, you couldn't do anything except listen for the bombs and hope that you would be spared.

The bombing was so heavy on this night that we dared not leave the shelter when the fires started. Bombs were coming down all around us ... the blast blew dust and sand into the shelter, even though the steel door was firmly closed. Our house was also hit by several incendiaries.

Eventually, we decided that we should try to get out ... . Some of the exits were blocked but we managed to get out into the street. Our house was well alight, the burning beams in the roof were falling down inside, into the next floor, the fire spreading steadily downwards ... .

That night changed all our lives. It wasn't just the material loss. There was the problem of finding a new home; my father caught pneumonia; my mother was in shock.

R. Nigmann quoted in M. Middlebrook, *The Berlin Raids*, Viking, New York, 1988, pp. 161–2.

DOCUMENT 17   DEATH OF A B-17

Despite its image as a 'Flying Fortress', the B-17, like all heavy bombers, was vulnerable to fighter attack. The following accounts describe the destruction of a Fortress during the disastrous Schweinfurt-Regensburg raid of October 1943 from the perspective of the attacking pilot and crew member inside a nearby B-17.

I side-slipped and levelled off just behind a bomber on which I had my sights, close enough to see the tail gunner inside. I pressed both buttons at once and all my guns fired. I saw a stream of fire going into the B-17 and that's all – except for one more thing. The Number 3 engine – the right-inner – actually came off the wing and whipped right back over me and the wing came off immediately afterwards. The bomber flipped onto its back.

....

I heard everyone hollering when the [German] fighters first came through ... . I suddenly saw the inboard engine on the right wing of the plane behind me come off. The whole engine came out and over the top of the wing, hit the right stabilizer and tore that off. The engine dropped out of sight. The plane flopped over completely and headed straight down. I saw no more; it went out of my sight but my assumption was that it went straight down like a bomb and buried itself ninety feet into the ground. You were supposed to count chutes but there was nothing to see on that one.

Accounts of Lt. E. Wagner [German fighter pilot] and Sgt. J. Johnson [American radio operator] quoted in M. Middlebrook, *The Schweinfurt-Regensburg Mission*, Scribner's, New York, 1983, pp. 206–7.

DOCUMENT 18   U-BOAT UNDER ATTACK

Even before the turn of the tide in the Battle of the Atlantic in the spring of 1943, German submarines were being sunk or – as the following account by the Captain of U-333 indicates – only narrowly escaping destruction.

Now it was 6 May 1942. I laid the boat on the bottom by the St. Lucie Shoal lighted whistle buoy in only 30 metres of water ... . Reloaded the tubes and started listening again ... . Lifted off the bottom and saw a steamer. But at the same time much finer sounds were reaching our ears at seconds' intervals: the ping-ping-ping-ping from the impulses of an Asdic sonar transmitting apparatus ... . They [US Coast Guard and USN vessels] were after me, had reached me at last. The attacker had become the quarry and now they set about despatching U 333 ... . I lowered the periscope and went at once to 20 metres, but before I got there the first depth charge crashed, making us stagger ... the hydroplanes failed ... the depth charges followed in series ... . Depth gauge and rudder indicator came loose, the engine-room telegraph broke ... trickles everywhere.

The minutes became eternity ... soon U 333 lay full length on the sea bed ... . Eventually the enemy would run out of ammunition. Until then we would have to keep our nerve. I tried to change our position and as gently as possible slip into deeper water. It seemed to succeed. Trimmed to nearly neutral buoyancy as far as circumstances allowed, with very little extra ballast and moving slowly, U 333 glided over the ocean floor. After seven hours (!) we at last reached 60 metres.

P. Cremer, *U-Boat Commander: A Periscope View of the Battle of the Atlantic*, Naval Institute Press, Annapolis, MY, 1984, pp. 72–4.

DOCUMENT 19   ON BEING SHELLED

One of the most frightening experiences for the modern infantryman is coming under sustained artillery fire. An extract from an 8th Army officer's diary for October 1942 indicates what it was like.

For the next half-hour we got a concentrated dose. It's most unpleasant crouching in the bottom of the pit, packed tight with even more chaps now whose single object is to keep their 'nuts' [heads] down as low as possible, silently braced and wondering whether the next one's coming our way. The shells scream down in inexorable succession, and all around us is the driving, rending crash of high explosive. Several times my tin-hat is crushed on to my head by the impact of nearby detonations, and once my lungs are filled by a rush of sand. Everyone lies still. You can't do a thing – it just has to happen. If one lands in the trench – well, we shan't know much about it.

R. L. Crimp, *The Diary of a Desert Rat*, Leo Cooper, London, 1971, p. 146.

DOCUMENT 20   GOEBBELS ON THE TURNING OF THE TIDE

By the spring of 1943 it was becoming evident even to hard-core supporters of Hitler such as Propaganda Minister Goebbels that the days of Nazi conquest were over.

Diary, 14 May 1943.
During the past five months the enemy has had the upper hand almost everywhere. He is defeating us in the air, he has inflicted heavy wounds on us in the East, he is beating us in North Africa, and even our submarine warfare is not so successful as we really expected it to be.

J. Goebbels [20], p. 379.

DOCUMENT 21   AMBUSH IN SICILY

Even though now on the defensive, the Wehrmacht *was often able to extract a high price for Allied advances. In his memoirs the Canadian novelist Farley Mowat recalled his first taste of the enemy while serving as an infantry officer during the invasion of Sicily.*

I heard a distant snarling bark, a whining scream, and then a stunning crash as a shell burst a few yards away from the carrier. Shrapnel and stone splinters sprayed against the vehicle's thin armour. It gave a skittish little leap, like a frightened horse, and slid sideways into the ditch ... .

Doc Macdonald grabbed my arm and together we rolled into the ditch behind the carrier. My other two sections [of Canadian infantry] had already abandoned their vehicles and were sprinting away from the road. Doc and I scrambled to our feet and joined the rout – just seconds before two of the carriers brewed up. *CRASH-Whooosh!* – *CRASH-Whooosh!* Their gasoline tanks flamed skyward and two immense black and golden globes blossomed over us ... .

From the crest and forward slopes of the mile-long escarpment the Germans were firing on us with everything they had – and they seemed to have just about everything.

....

'Mother of God, what's that!' Doc yelled as an ear-splitting whiplash of sound ended in a savage crunch that showered us with grit and gravel.

I had already heard that one, for it had been the nemesis of our carrier. It was the infamous Eighty-eight [mm anti-aircraft/anti-tank gun] ... In days to come its very name would become freighted with acute apprehension ... .

By now our column had recovered somewhat from the first shock of ambush and was beginning to fight back. The British Priests [self-propelled guns] deployed and soon the throaty roar of their 25-pounders firing over open sights was followed by a familiar snarl as their shells tunneled over us to erupt in bursts of flame along the escarpment. The reserve squadron of Shermans rattled forward, went into hull-down positions behind some little knolls, and the wicked bark of their 75's joined the swelling din. Even we of the infantry, now scattered in little groups over the flat plain, began to reply with rifle and Bren [machine gun] fire aimed in the general direction of the unseen enemy.

F. Mowat, *And No Birds Sang*, Bantam-Seal, New York, 1981, pp. 98–101.

DOCUMENT 22   **SUMMARY JUSTICE ON THE EASTERN FRONT**

One of the reasons the Wehrmacht *did not collapse in the face of overwhelming enemy force was the ferocious discipline imposed on it by military police and the SS. The standard penalty for unauthorized withdrawals was death. The following scene, recounted by a former Waffen-SS man, was far from uncommon.*

June 29 [1944]. '*SS Kontrolle! Halt ... !*'

All military trucks and cars heading west are checked on the Mohilev-Minsk road.

Those officers and men who cannot produce written orders to prove that they are on duty are ruthlessly shot ... .

A Mercedes, camouflaged with branches, stops at our roadblock. A captain and two other officers are in the car. Judging by their white faces, they must have realized what this is all about.

About forty SS, in black helmets, are lined up on both sides of the road, machine-guns at the ready ...

I walk up to them and salute.

'SS Control! Your movement order, please!'

The captain takes a piece of paper from his tunic pocket and hands it to me. I look at it and hand it back to him.

'I'm sorry *Herr Hauptmann*. This is your front-line identification permit. I said your movement order. Is this all you can show me?'

Abject fear is written all over the faces of the three men. They are obviously Staff Officers who, having no effective command, must have decided to head for Minsk off their own bats. But at a time when all our resources should be mustered to try to hold the Bolsheviks, it is neither more nor less than treason to run away without fighting.

Stressling now walks up.

'Get out of that car in double-quick time!'

The three men get out. An SS man climbs in immediately, and parks the car on the far side of the road.

'Your papers, gentlemen!' says Stressling, his face hard.

He reads them carefully, then looks up.

'Ninth Army Staff? What are you doing here, on this road?'

'We were going to Minsk, *Herr Major*.'

'*Sturmbannführer* to you!' roars Stressling. 'Oh, so you were going to Minsk, were you? Well, I don't believe you'll get there!'

'But you have no right to ... '

'Oh, so I've no right?'

He signals to me.

'Neumann! Liquidate this bunch of traitors!'

A few moments later the three Staff Officers are led into a field, off the road ... .

P. Neumann, *Other Men's Graves*, Weidenfeld and Nicolson, London, 1958, pp. 244–5.

DOCUMENT 23   ALLIED VS. GERMAN TANKS

The following conversation between two British tank officers in Normandy is partly apocryphal but accurately conveys the marked inferiority of Allied armour in Normandy.

'What do the Germans have most of?'
'Panthers. The Panther can slice through a Churchill like butter from a mile away.'
'And how does a Churchill get a Panther?'
'It creeps up on it. When it reaches close quarters the gunner tries to bounce a shot off the underside of the Panther's gun mantlet. If he's lucky it goes through a piece of thin armour above the driver's head.'
'Has anybody ever done it?'
'Yes, Davis of C Squadron. He's back with headquarters now, trying to recover his nerve.'
'How does a Churchill get a Tiger?'
'He's supposed to get within two hundred yards and put a shot through the periscope.'
'Has anyone ever done it?'
'No.'

A. A. Wilson, *Flame Thrower*, George Mann, Maidstone, 1974, p. 54.

DOCUMENT 24   AIRPOWER OVER NORMANDY

One of the keys to Allied success in Normandy was control of the skies. Kurt Meyer, a Waffen-SS commander, recalled the problems Allied fighter-bombers caused.

Field Marshal Rommel … asks me for an appreciation of the situation. I reply … 'The enemy's overwhelming command of the air makes tactical manoeuvre virtually impossible. The fighter bombers even attack individual dispatch riders. Redeployment of the smallest units, let alone massed concentrations, can not be carried out without serious losses because of continuous air surveillance. The road network is under their control day and night. A few fighter bombers are enough to delay or even stop movements. Field Marshal, give us an air umbrella, give us some fighter units! We are not afraid of the enemy ground forces, [but] we are powerless against the concentrated air operations.'
    It would have been better not to have made that last request. I see that I have touched a sensitive area. The Field Marshal says excitedly, 'Why are you telling me this? Do you believe that I drive around with my eyes closed? I have written report after report. In Africa I drew attention to the fatal impact of the fighter bombers, but the gentlemen [Hitler's staff], of course, know much better. They simply don't believe my reports any longer!' …

The Field Marshal takes a few minutes' stroll before he bids me a fond farewell, Sepp Dietrich [senior *Waffen-SS* commander] asks the Field Marshal to be careful and avoid the main road. ... The Field Marshal drives away. He is attacked and wounded shortly afterwards near Foy de Montgomery.

K. Meyer, *Grenadiers*, Fedorowicz, Winnipeg, MN, 1994, pp. 152–3.

DOCUMENT 25   THE COMMANDANT OF AUSCHWITZ
INTERVIEWED

As the US staff psychologist during the Nuremberg war crimes trials discovered, those responsible for carrying out the Holocaust often regarded their task as a technical challenge rather than a moral dilemma.

I asked [Colonel Rudolf] Hoess how it was technically possible to exterminate $2\frac{1}{2}$ million people. 'Technically?' he asked. 'That wasn't so hard – it would not have been hard to exterminate even greater numbers.' ... it was possible to exterminate up to 10,000 people in one 24-hour period. ... 'The killing itself took the least time ... it was the burning that took all the time. The killing was easy; you didn't even need guards to drive them into the chambers; they just went in expecting to take showers and, instead of water, we turned on poison gas. The whole thing went very quickly.' He related all this in a quiet, apathetic, matter-of-fact tone of voice.

I was interested in finding out how the order had actually been given and what his reactions were. He related it as follows: 'In the summer of 1941, Himmler called for me and explained: "The Führer has ordered the *Endlösung* [final solution] of the Jewish question – and we have to carry out the task. For reasons of transportation and isolation, I have picked Auschwitz for this. You now have the job of carrying this out." As a reason for this he said that it would have to be done at this time, because if it was not done now, then the Jew would later exterminate the German people – or words to that effect. For this reason one had to ignore all human considerations and consider only the task – or words to that effect.' I asked him whether he didn't express any opinion on the subject or show any reluctance. 'I had nothing to say; I could only say *Jawohl*!' ... 'But what about the human – ?' I started to ask.

'That just didn't enter into it,' was the pat answer before I could finish the question.

G. M. Gilbert, *Nuremberg Diary*, Farrar, Strauss, New York, 1947, pp. 249–51.

CHRONOLOGY OF EVENTS

1939   Sept. 1, Germany invades Poland.
Sept. 3, Britain and France declare war on Germany.
Sept. 7, USSR invades eastern Poland.
Sept. 28, Warsaw falls.
Sept. 30, Germany and USSR divide Poland.
Nov. 3, USA allows Britain and France to buy arms on 'cash and carry' basis.
Nov. 30, USSR attacks Finland.

1940   Mar. 12, Finland signs peace treaty with USSR, ceding territory.
Apr. 9, Germany invades Denmark and Norway.
Apr. 14, British forces land in Norway.
May 2, British forces evacuated from Norway.
May 10, Chamberlain replaced by Churchill as British prime minister.
German attack in the West begins.
May 14, Main German drive through Sedan area begins.
Dutch surrender.
May 28, Belgian surrender.
May 29 – June 3, Evacuation of BEF from Continent via Dunkirk.
June 10, Italy declares war on France and Britain.
June 17–23, USSR occupies Baltic states.
June 22, France under Pétain enters into Armistice with Germany.
July 3, French fleet attacked by British at Mers-el-Kébir.
July–Sept, Battle of Britain.
Aug., Blitz begins.
Oct. 12, German invasion of Britain cancelled by Hitler.
Oct. 28, Italy begins invasion attempt against Greece.
Nov. 11, Italian fleet at Taranto successfully attacked by British carrier-based aircraft.
Dec., Italian reverses in North Africa.

1941   Jan., Further Italian reverses in North Africa.
Feb., German forces under Rommel sent to assist Italians in North Africa.

Mar. 11, Lend-Lease bill passes US Congress.
Mar. – May, German offensive in North Africa drives British back.
May 20, Italian surrender in Abyssinia.
Apr., Germany invades Yugoslavia and Greece.
Apr. 28, Last British forces evacuated from Greece.
May 20–31, German airborne invasion of Crete.
June 22, Operation Barbarossa – German invasion of USSR – begins.
July, Destruction of Jews begins.
Aug. 11, Atlantic Charter signed by Churchill and Roosevelt.
Sept. 30, Germans begin drive on Moscow.
Nov. – Dec., British offensive drives back Rommel in Libya.
Dec. 5, Red Army launches Moscow counteroffensive.
Dec. 7–11, Japan and USA enter war; Germany and Italy declare war on USA.

1942
Jan., Rommel begins new advance towards Egypt.
Feb. 6, Anglo-American Combined Chiefs of Staff (CCS) created.
May, Soviet offensive in Kharkov region defeated.
May 20, Lend-Lease extended to USSR.
May 30, First 1,000 bomber raid by RAF Bomber Command (Cologne).
June, German summer offensive in southern USSR begins.
Sept. 5, Germans enter Stalingrad.
Oct., Rommel defeated at El Alamein and forced to retreat towards Tripoli.
Nov., Allies land and occupy French North Africa. Germans occupy Vichy France.
Nov. 19, Soviet counteroffensive at Stalingrad begins.

1943
Jan. 14–24, Casablanca conference.
Jan. 31 – Feb. 2, German Sixth Army in Stalingrad surrenders.
Apr., Russo-Polish friction over Katyn massacre.
May 12, German forces in North Africa surrender at Tunis.
May, Turning-point in Battle of the Atlantic.
May 27, Hamburg firestorm (RAF).
June 4, Committee of National Liberation formed under De Gaulle.
July, Germans defeated in Kursk offensive.
Allies invade Sicily.
Sept., Allies land in southern Italy; Italian surrender; German occupation.
Nov. 6, Red Army takes Kiev.
Nov. 28 – Dec. 1, Tehran conference.

1944   Jan. 22, Allied landing at Anzio in Italy.
        Jan. 27, Relief of Leningrad by Red Army.
        Feb. 20–27, Big Week (sustained USAAF and RAF bombing of
            German aircraft industry)
        Feb. – Mar., Monte Cassino battles in Italy.
        Apr. 2, Red Army enters Romania.
        June 6, D-Day landings.
        June 23, Major Soviet summer offensive (Bagration) opens.
        June – Aug., Battle for Normandy.
        July 20, Failed German attempt to assassinate Hitler.
        July 26, Moscow recognizes Lublin Poles.
        Aug. 11, Allied landings in south of France.
        Aug. 1, Warsaw Uprising begins.
        Aug. 30, Red Army enters Bucharest.
        Sept. 5, British and Canadian troops enter Brussels.
        Sept. 17–25, Allied airborne offensive through Arnhem fails.
        Sept. 19, Finns sign Armistice with USSR.
        Oct. 3, Warsaw Uprising ends.
        Dec. 17, Battle of the Bulge begins.

1945   Jan. 3, Allied counter-attack in Ardennes begins.
        Jan. 17, Red Army enters Warsaw.
        Feb. 4–11, Yalta conference.
        Feb. 13, Fall of Budapest to Red Army.
        Destruction of Dresden by RAF.
        Mar. – Apr., Crossing of Rhine by Allied forces.
        Apr. 20, Red Army forces penetrate into Berlin.
        Apr. 28, Mussolini killed by partisans.
        Apr. 30, Hitler commits suicide.
        May 2, Berlin surrenders to Red Army.
        May 8, VE Day.

GLOSSARY

Abwehr   German military intelligence organization.

Afrika Korps   Official term for German forces fighting in North Africa under Rommel, 1941–43.

Atlantic Charter   The declaration of broad Allied war aims signed by Roosevelt and Churchill in August 1941.

Atlantic Wall   Grandiose Nazi title given to the German shore defences along the French coast to protect against Allied invasion, 1943–44.

Axis   The term, derived from the agreement signed by Mussolini and Hitler in 1936, most commonly used to denote collectively the nations fighting the Allies, principally Germany, Italy, and Japan.

B-17 Flying Fortress   Heavily armed US four-engine bomber, the mainstay of the USAAF strategic bombing campaign.

B-24 Liberator   US four-engine aircraft used both in strategic bombing and anti-submarine operations.

Bagration   Code name for the main Soviet summer offensive, 1944.

Barbarossa   Code name for the German plan to invade the western USSR and defeat the Red Army before the end of 1941. After spectacular successes from June onward the German invasion forces ground to a halt outside Moscow in November with the Red Army severely mauled but not destroyed.

BEF   The British Expeditionary Force, the army sent to help defend France against invasion in 1939–40 that was forced to evacuate from Dunkirk in late May 1940.

Bf-109   Single-seat, single-engine fighter of prewar design, built by Messerschmitt. The mainstay of the *Luftwaffe*'s fighter arm throughout the war (supplemented after 1941 by the Focke-Wulf 190).

Blitz Popular name for the German night bombing of British cities, especially London, 1940–41.

Blitzkrieg The popular term ('lightning war') for the co-ordinated and speedy use of armour and air power in deep penetration offensives pioneered by the *Wehrmacht* in the early years of the war.

Blue Code name for the 1942 German summer offensive in the south on the Eastern Front.

Bomber Command The arm of the RAF responsible for strategic and other bombing.

Casablanca Conference The January 1943 meeting in which Churchill and Roosevelt, along with their military staffs, argued over future moves and ultimately agreed to the postponement of a cross-Channel invasion in favour of a Mediterranean strategy for 1943. The defeat of the U-boats and the intensification of the bombing of Germany were also made priorities.

CCS Combined Chiefs of Staff, the organization which effectively pooled the talents of the US Joint Chiefs of Staff and the British Chiefs of Staff.

Chetniks Resistance movement in Yugoslavia led by General Mihailovic that turned collaborationist in 1941–42 and fought Tito's Partisans.

Citadel Code name for what turned out to be the last German strategic offensive on the Eastern Front, launched at Kursk in July 1943, and ending in complete victory for the Red Army.

Commissars Red Army political officers.

Cromwell Developed from earlier British cruiser tank designs in 1943, both its armour and gun were weak in comparison to many of the German tanks it fought in Normandy in 1944.

Duce Title assumed by Mussolini as head of the Fascist Party and leader of the Italian state.

Enigma An enciphering machine much used by the Germans in radio traffic.

FFI The interior resistance army of the Free French movement.

Fighter Command The arm of the RAF devoted to air defence.

Final Solution   Nazi euphemism for the destruction of the European Jews.

Fortitude   Code name for the Allied deception operations designed to make the Germans think the Allied invasion of France in 1944 was destined for the Pas-de-Calais.

Führer   Hitler's title as head of the Nazi Party and German Reich.

Geneva Convention   The 1929 international agreement concerning the proper treatment of wounded and captured enemy personnel.

Gestapo   German secret police organization.

Gothic Line   German defensive positions across northern Italy that proved difficult to overcome in late 1944–45.

GRU   Soviet military intelligence organization.

Gustav Line   Series of German defensive positions across Italy south of Rome, breached with some difficulty by Allied forces in early 1944.

Hedgehog   Name given to the forward-firing anti-submarine depth bomb system introduced in British and Canadian escort ships beginning in 1941.

HF/DF   High frequency radio direction finding system installed on British and Allied escort vessels from 1942 onward, enabling them to home in on U-boat radio transmissions.

Home Army   The Polish underground force linked with the Polish government in exile which rose up unsuccessfully against the Germans in Warsaw in late 1944.

Hurricane   Single-seat, single-engine fighter of prewar design, obsolescent by 1941–42 but along with the Spitfire the mainstay of RAF Fighter Command in the Battle of Britain.

Husky   Code name for the Allied invasion of Sicily, July 1943.

Il-2 Stormovik   Rugged, armoured, and heavily armed single-engine Soviet ground attack aircraft.

Katyn Massacre   The murder of over a thousand Polish officers in the Katyn forest by Soviet security forces in 1940. Mass graves, discovered by the Germans in 1943, were used as anti-Soviet propaganda. It was the superficial cause of the breaking off of relations between the London Poles and Moscow, though the major Allies continued to support the Soviet line that the Nazis were responsible.

Kriegsmarine The German navy.

Lancaster The most successful four-engine British bomber of the war and the mainstay of Bomber Command operations in the second half of the war.

Lend Lease System through which the United States provided, within the law, virtually free material aid to Britain and later the USSR.

Liberty Ship Mass-produced, prefabricated US cargo vessel.

London Poles Term used to denote the Polish government-in-exile based in London.

Lublin Poles Term used to denote the communist puppet group created by Stalin in 1944 that formed the basis of the postwar communist regime in Poland.

Luftwaffe German air force.

Maginot Line Series of elaborate French fortifications built along the Franco-German border in the early 1930s.

Maquis The French resistance bands based in the hills of southern France, 1942–44.

Market-Garden Code name for the Allied combined ground and airborne offensive to seize key river crossings in Holland, September 1944.

Me-163 German rocket fighter built by Messerschmitt in 1944–45. The small number deployed to counter the USAAF over Germany proved fast but highly dangerous to fly.

Me-262 Twin-engine German jet fighter built by Messerschmitt, available in too small quantities to alter the balance of air power over Europe in 1944–45.

MI6 The British Secret Intelligence Service.

Milice French collaborationist paramilitary organization in league with the Germans against the Resistance.

New Order Term for the reordering of Europe under Nazi rule.

NKVD Soviet intelligence, counterintelligence, and political secret police organization.

OKW   German armed forces high command.

OSS   Office of Strategic Services, the US intelligence agency set up in 1942 which combined intelligence gathering with support for resistance activity.

Overlord   Code name for the planned Allied landings in Normandy, June 1944.

Panther   Advanced German medium tank introduced in 1943 to counter the T-34, and greatly superior to most American and British tanks in 1944–45.

Partisans   The name given to members of communist guerilla forces behind German lines, especially in Russia and Yugoslavia.

P-47 Thunderbolt   Large US single-engine, single-seat fighter which, along with the P-51, served as the mainstay of USAAF fighter and later ground attack operations over Europe.

P-51 Mustang   US single-engine, single-seat fighter which, when equipped with a powerful British engine in 1942 and later drop tanks, became a highly effective bomber escort.

Potsdam Conference   The final Big Three summit of the war in July 1945 (Stalin, Truman, Churchill/Attlee) in which the partition of Germany and the future of Eastern Europe in general were planned. The split between Stalin and the Western Powers, already evident at Yalta, became obvious at Potsdam.

Radar   Radio detection and ranging system first developed as a ground-based way to find aircraft but soon deployed on ships and in aircraft as well in smaller and increasingly sophisticated forms variously to identify aircraft, ships, and other targets.

RAF   The (British) Royal Air Force.

RCN   Royal Canadian Navy.

Regia Aeronautica   Italian air force.

SD   German counter intelligence organization, part of Himmler's SS empire.

Sealion   The operational plan for the 1940 German invasion of England, called off after the defeat of the *Luftwaffe* in the Battle of Britain.

Second Front   The Allied cross-Channel invasion, postponed in 1942 and again in 1943, which Stalin repeatedly demanded from the Western Allies in order to relieve pressure on the Eastern Front.

Sherman US medium tank. Useful in North Africa in 1942, by 1943–44 it was outclassed by the latest German designs but remained the mainstay of American (and to some extent British) armoured forces.

Siegfried Line Prewar German fortifications facing the French Maginot Line. Not maintained after the German victories of 1940, they were hastily refurbished as invasion from the west became likely again in the autumn of 1944.

Sonar Acoustic echo detection system employed by surface ships to detect submerged submarines.

SOE Special Operations Executive, the clandestine British organization set up in 1940 to co-ordinate resistance activity in Occupied Europe.

Spitfire Single-engine, single-seat fighter of prewar design that evolved into the most successful British fighter of the war.

Squid Forward-throwing anti-submarine depth charge mortar system introduced in late 1943 in Allied escort vessels as a successor to the lighter Hedgehog.

SS Nazi paramilitary organization which became the dominant arm of the Nazi state apparatus.

Stavka Acronym for the Red Army general staff.

T-34 Soviet medium tank which became the mainstay of Soviet armoured forces.

Tiger German heavy tank introduced in 1943 to counter Soviet armour. Less well armed and armoured Allied tanks found it very difficult to knock out.

Torch Code name for the Allied invasion of (Vichy) French North Africa launched in November 1942.

U-Boat German submarine, typically the Type VIIC.

Ultra The code name for the highly secret information British cryptanalysts based at Bletchley Park were able to glean from decoded German enigma messages.

Unconditional Surrender The Allied policy announced by Roosevelt at Casablanca in January 1943 that there would be no negotiated peace with the Axis powers.

Uranus   Code name for the Soviet counter offensive at Stalingrad, November 1942.

USAAF   The United States Army Air Forces.

USN   United States Navy.

USSR   Union of Soviet Socialist Republics (i.e. Soviet Union).

V-1   German pulse-jet powered flying bomb, fired in quantity against London and later Antwerp with limited success in 1944–45.

V-2   German ballistic missile fired from mobile launchers in 1944–45, aimed mostly against London.

Vichy   Term used to denote the post-armistice French government led by Marshal Pétain.

Volkssturm   German people's militia formed in 1944–45 from old men and youngsters.

Waffen-SS   The military arm of the SS, the size and power of which grew during the war in proportion to Hitler's disillusionment with the *Wehrmacht*.

Wehrmacht   Term used for the German armed forces after Hitler's rise to power, but used more commonly to denote the army alone.

WINDOW   Code name for the aluminium-coated strips first dropped by British night bombers, 1943, to confuse German radar.

Wolf Pack   The tactic pioneered by Dönitz involving the convergence of a number of U-boats on a sighted convoy before an attack was launched so as to swamp the convoy defences.

Yak-9   Soviet fighter introduced in late 1942, and along with the Yak-3 of 1943 the most successful in a series of Soviet single-engine, single-seat fighters built by Yakovlev.

Yalta Conference   The acrimonious meeting of Churchill, Roosevelt and Stalin in February 1945 in which Soviet participation in the war against Japan and the future of Poland were among the subjects discussed.

GUIDE TO CHARACTERS

Arnim, General Jürgen von (1891–1971): Sent to command Axis forces based on Tunis in November 1942, he replaced Rommel as overall commander in March 1943, two months before the final Allied victory in North Africa.

Arnold, General Henry H. (1886–1956): Commander of the USAAF. A strong believer in independent airpower and the US strategic bombing effort.

Attlee, Clement (1883–1967): Leader of the British Labour Party and level-headed deputy Prime Minister, 1940–45, he succeeded Churchill as Prime Minister after the General Election of July 1945.

Auchinleck, General Sir Claude (1884–1981): Succeeded Wavell as commander of British forces in the Middle East in November 1941. His mixed record of success and failure in fighting Rommel while directing the 8th Army in the Western Desert led to his transfer by Churchill in August 1942.

Badoglio, Marshal Pietro (1871–1956): Italian soldier and politician. He headed the Italian government after the overthrow of Mussolini (July 1943), negotiated an armistice with the Allies (September 1943), and declared war on Germany (October 1943). He resigned in June 1944.

Bradley, General Omar (1893–1981): After serving in North Africa and Sicily he rose to command the US 1st Army during the D-Day landings and later the 12th Army Group in the campaign for Northwest Europe, 1944–45. Arguably the best senior US ground commander (and certainly the least arrogant) in the European Theatre of Operations.

Chamberlain, Neville (1860–1940): British Prime Minister, 1937–1940, and chief architect of Appeasement. He resigned after a no-confidence vote in the House of Commons, 10 May 1940, following British defeat in the Norway campaign, and was replaced by Churchill.

Churchill, Winston (1874–1964): Heroic Prime Minister of Britain, 1940–45, and leading statesman in the Allied coalition. Though his grasp of operational realities was sometimes weak, he understood the supreme value of American friendship and did much to promote British interests. Perhaps best known for rallying resistance to Hitler in 1940.

Clark, General Mark (1896–1984): Commander of the US 5th Army and 15th Army Group in the Italian campaign. The quality of his generalship has been the subject of debate.

Daladier, Edouard (1884–1970): Cautious, more-or-less pro-appeasement Premier of France, April 1938 to March 1940, whose lacklustre performance in the first months of the war led to his resignation and replacement by the more energetic Paul Reynaud.

Dönitz, Grand Admiral Karl (1891–1980): Wartime commander of the U-boat fleet and (from 1943 onward) chief of the German navy. A superb tactician and believer in the strategic role of the U-boat whose expanding submarine force came close to victory in the Battle of the Atlantic in 1942–43. His political loyalty was repaid when Hitler named him his successor in April 1945.

Dowding, Air Chief Marshal Sir Hugh (1882–1970): Headed RAF Fighter Command, 1936–40. His tactical leadership during the Battle of Britain helped ensure that the *Luftwaffe* was defeated and Britain allowed to fight on.

Eisenhower, General Dwight D. (1890–1969): Supreme Commander Allied Expedionary Forces, 1943–45 and later President of the United States. His administrative abilities and, above all, his personal skills did much to keep Anglo-American relations smooth and Allied strategy in Europe both before and after the Normandy invasion coherent.

Frank, Hans (1900–46): The extremely brutal Nazi Governor-General of occupied Poland. He was hanged as a war criminal in 1946.

Gamelin, General Maurice (1872–1958): French Commander-in-Chief 1939–40. His performance in the Battle of France did not match his high prewar reputation.

de Gaulle, General Charles (1890–1970): Leader of the Free French resistance movement based in London, and subsequently leader of the French provisional government. Arrogant and intolerant but possessed of a strong sense of mission, he took a stand against both the Germans and Vichy in 1940 when few other Frenchmen were willing to fight on.

Goebbels, Josef (1897–1945): Reich propaganda minister. A master of mass communication and a skilled orator, he did much to rally public support for total war in the years of German defeat.

Goering, Hermann (1893–1946): Commander of the German air force. His leadership skills and political influence declined progressively after 1941. He was hanged as a war criminal at Nuremberg.

Gort, Field-Marshal Lord (1886–1946): Commander of the BEF in 1940. A brave but not brilliant general.

Harris, Air Chief Marshal Sir Arthur (1892–1984): A true believer in strategic bombing and the architect of RAF Bomber Command's area bombing strategy against German cities, 1942–1945.

Hitler, Adolf (1889–1945): Führer of the Third Reich and chief instigator of both the Second World War and Holocaust. His military judgement deteriorated sharply as the war progressed.

Kesselring, Field-Marshal Albert (1885–1960): *Luftwaffe* general best known for his skilful direction and defensive deployment of German forces during the Italian Campaign, 1943–45. Among the best German field commanders of the war.

Konev, Marshal Ivan (1897–1973): Successful Red Army commander, rivalling Zhukov in skill.

Lindemann, Professor Frederick (1886–1957): Chief scientific advisor to Winston Churchill. His judgements – often based on statistical models – were not always accurate.

Manstein, Field Marshal Erich von (1887–1973): German commander responsible for the plan which led to German success in the Battle of France and notable tactical triumphs on the Eastern Front. Arguably the most outstanding German planner and field general of the war.

Marshall, General George C. (1880–1959): Immensely capable Chairman of the US Joint Chiefs of Staff. He oversaw the massive expansion of US forces from 1940 onward and played a key role in the formulation of Allied grand strategy.

Mihailovic, General Draza (1893–1946): Leader of the Chetnik resistance movement in Yugoslavia. His desire to avoid civilian bloodshed led him to begin collaborating with the Germans in 1942, which in turn led the British to switch their support to Tito and the Partisans in 1943.

Model, Field-Marshal Walther (1891–1945):   Known as 'The Führer's Fireman', his loyalty to Hitler and skill in shoring up crumbling defences combined to place him in a series of important but doomed senior commands in 1944–45. He shot himself in April 1945.

Montgomery, Field-Marshal Sir Bernard (1887–1976):   Commander of the British 8th Army during operations in North Africa, Sicily, and Italy, 1942–43, and subsequently in charge of D-Day ground operations and 21st Army Group in the campaign for Northwest Europe, 1944–45. Methodical and thorough but also arrogant, he related poorly with his American counterparts.

Mussert, Anton (1894–1946):   Dutch Nazi leader. Installed by Berlin in 1942 as leader in the Netherlands, he never achieved any real independence from his German masters.

Mussolini, Benito (1883–1945):   Italian dictator. Responsible for bringing Fascist Italy into the war and for a succession of poor strategic decisions. In July 1943 he was overthrown, but rescued and reinstated with Hitler's support in German-occupied Italy. Killed by Italian partisans, April 1945.

Patton, General George (1885–1945):   Commander of US 1st Corps in Tunisia, the US 7th Army in Sicily, and the US 1st Army in Northwest Europe. Hard-driving and flamboyant, he consistently maintained pressure on enemy forces and was a master of exploitation.

Paulus, Field-Marshal Friedrich von (1890–1957):   Ill-fated commander of the German 6th Army during the Battle of Stalingrad. Against Hitler's orders he surrendered what was left of his encircled army in January 1943, and later broadcast anti-Nazi propaganda for the Russians.

Pétain, Marshal Phillipe (1856–1951):   Aged leader of Vichy France. His accommodationist stance towards the Nazi New Order ultimately proved counter-productive.

Quisling, Vidkun (1887–1945):   Puppet leader of a pro-German government installed after the German occupation of Norway. His name quickly became a synonym for turncoat behaviour.

Reynaud, Paul (1878–1966):   Premier of France during the German invasion of 1940, his natural combativeness could not compensate for the weaknesses of the French forces.

Rokossovsky, Marshal Konstantin (1896–1968):   Soviet front commander in a series of important Red Army battles from Stalingrad onward. One of the great Red Army field commanders of the war.

Rommel, Field-Marshal Erwin (1891–1944): Commander of the Afrika Korps, 1941–43, and in partial command of the German forces facing the Allied invasion in Normandy, 1944. An outstanding leader and tactician, his victories were always offset by logistical difficulties which prevented proper exploitation. He was (falsely) suspected of complicity in the July Bomb Plot and forced to commit suicide in October 1944.

Roosevelt, Franklin D. (1882–1944): President of the United States, 1932–45, and US Commander-in-Chief during the war. His political acumen and ability to judge the long-range threat posed by Nazi Germany to US interests helped ensure that Britain received much needed aid in 1940–41 and that the war in Europe received priority over the war against Japan once America had formally entered the conflict.

Rundstedt, Field Marshal Karl von (1875–1953): Commander of key German forces in the Battle of France, Operation Barbarossa, the opening phase of the Normandy campaign, and the Ardennes Offensive. An ageing but highly efficient Prussian professional.

Spaatz, General Carl (1891–1974): Commander of the US 8th Air Force based in Britain and later all US strategic air forces in Europe. A strong believer in the efficacy of strategic bombing.

Speer, Albert (1905–1982): Reich Minister for Armaments and Production, 1942–45. A man of considerable administrative ability, he was able to significantly boost German arms production in the second half of the war.

Stalin, Joseph (1879–1953): Soviet dictator and wartime generalissimo. His strategic decisions in 1941–42 helped ensure defeat for the Red Army, but he learned from his mistakes and allowed professional advice to govern military actions in later years. Responsible for the extension of Soviet hegemony into Eastern Europe in 1944–45.

Timoshenko, Marshal Semion (1895–1970): One of the few commanders to emerge comparatively unscathed from the Red Army disasters of 1941, he proved unable to deliver the victory Stalin wanted in the Kharkov offensive in May 1942.

Tito, Josip Broz (1892–1980): Leader of the successful communist-led Partisan resistance movement in Yugoslavia. His determination to fight the Germans at whatever cost earned him British support from 1943 onwards.

Vasilevsky, Marshal Aleksander (1895–1977): Stavka chief, 1942–45, who spent much of the time in the field. One of the Red Army's greatest wartime commanders.

Wavell, General Sir Archibald (1883–1950):   Commander of British Forces in the Middle East, 1939–1941. His success in overseeing the defeat of Italian forces in Africa in 1940 was overshadowed by setbacks – mostly not of his making – in Greece, Crete, and the Western Desert in 1941. Churchill replaced him with Auchinleck in November.

Weygand, General Maxime (1867–1965):   Brought in to replace Gamelin in May 1940 during the Battle of France, he proved unable to stem the German tide despite greater vigour than his predecessor. He supported Pétain's call for an armistice and was briefly a Vichy minister.

Zhukov, Marshal Georgi (1896–1974):   Brutal but effective senior Red Army commander, responsible for a series of Soviet victories from the defence of Moscow (1941–42) to the battle for Berlin (1945). Arguably the greatest Red Army general of the war.

BIBLIOGRAPHY

The number of works on the Second World War in English alone is legion. The following list of books is therefore a necessarily subjective, but hopefully representative, sample of a much larger body of literature, with emphasis on material published within the last twenty years (the major exception being works cited for historiographical purposes in the analysis section). Readers should note, however, that much can be gleaned from earlier material, including the British and American official histories.

GUIDES

1   Dear, I. C. B. (ed.), *The Oxford Companion to World War II*, Oxford UP, Oxford, 1995.
2   Enser, A. G. S., *A Subject Bibliography of the Second World War: Books in English, 1975–1987*, Gower, London, 1990.
3   Funk, A. L., *The Second World War: A Select Bibliography of Books in English since 1975*, Regina Books, Claremont, CA, 1985.
4   Higham, R. (ed.), *Official Military Histories*, Greenwood, Westport, CT, 1997.
5   Keegan, J., *The Battle for History: Re-Fighting World War II*, Vintage, Toronto, 1995.
6   Lee, L. E. (ed.), *World War II in Europe, Africa, and the Americas, with General Sources: A Handbook of Literature and Research*, Greenwood, Westport, CT, 1997.

GENERAL ACCOUNTS

7   Calvocoressi, P., G. Wint, J. Pritchard, *Total War*, 2nd edn, Pantheon Books, New York, 1989.
8   Fuller, J. F. C., *The Second World War, 1939–45*, Meredith, New York, 1948.
9   Gilbert, M., *The Second World War*, Weidenfeld and Nicolson, London, 1989.
10 Keegan, J., *The Second World War*, Viking, New York, 1990.

11   Kitchen, M., *A World in Flames*, Longmans, London, 1990.
12   Lee, L. E., *The War Years*, Unwin Hyman, Boston, 1989.
13   Liddell Hart, B. H., *History of the Second World War*, Cassell, London, 1970.
14   Parker, R. A. C., *The Second World War*, Oxford UP paperback edn, Oxford, 1997.
15   Weinberg, G. L., *A World at Arms*, Cambridge UP, Cambridge, 1994.
16   Willmott, H. P., *The Great Crusade*, Macmillan, London, 1989.

MEMOIRS AND CONTEMPORARY SOURCES

17   Badoglio, P., *Italy in the Second World War: Memoirs and Documents*, Oxford UP, London, 1948.
18   Bland, L. I. (ed.), *The Papers of George Catlett Marshall*, vols. 2–4, Johns Hopkins UP, Baltimore, 1986–96.
19   Churchill, W. S. C., *The Second World War*, 6 vols, Houghton Mifflin, Boston, 1948–53.
20   Goebbels, J., *The Goebbels Diaries, 1942–1943*, Garden City, Garden City, NY, 1948.
21   de Gaulle, C., *The War Memoirs*, Viking, New York, 1955.
22   Hitler, A., *Hitler's Table Talk, 1941–44*, 2nd edn, Weidenfeld and Nicolson, London, 1973.
23   International Military Tribunal, *Trial of the German Major War Criminals*, 23 vols, HMSO, 1946–49.
24   Kimball, R. M. (ed.), *Churchill & Roosevelt: The Complete Correspondence*, 3 vols, Princeton UP, Princeton, NJ, 1984.
25   Speer, A., *Inside the Third Reich*, Avon Books, New York, 1970.
26   Zhukov, G. K., *The Memoirs of Marshal Zhukov*, Delacorte, New York, 1971.

BIOGRAPHIES

27   Ambrose, S., *Eisenhower*, vol. 1, Simon and Schuster, New York, 1983.
28   Barnett, C. (ed.), *Hitler's Generals*, Weidenfeld and Nicolson, London, 1989.
29   Bullock, A., *Hitler and Stalin*, HarperCollins, London, 1991.
30   D'Este, C., *Patton*, HarperCollins, New York, 1995.
31   Fraser, D., *Knight's Cross: A Life of Field Marshal Erwin Rommel*, HarperCollins, London, 1993.
32   Granatstein, J. L., *The Generals: The Canadian Army's Senior Commanders in the Second World War*, Stoddart, Toronto, 1993.
33   Hamilton, N., *Monty*, 3 vols, Hamish Hamilton, London, 1981–86.
34   Keegan, J. (ed.), *Churchill's Generals*, Weidenfeld and Nicolson, London, 1991.

35   Kimball, W. F., *The Juggler: Franklin Roosevelt as Wartime Statesman*, Princeton UP, Princeton, 1991.
36   Lamb, R., *Churchill as War Leader*, Bloomsbury, London, 1991.
37   Lacouture, J., *Charles de Gaulle*, vol. 1, Norton, New York, 1990.
38   Mack Smith, D., *Mussolini*, Knopf, New York, 1982.
39   Shukman, H. (ed.), *Stalin's Generals*, Weidenfeld and Nicolson, London, 1993.
40   Volkogonov, D., *Stalin: Triumph and Tragedy*, Prima, Rocklin, CA, 1992.

ORIGINS/PREPAREDNESS

41   Alexander, M., *The Republic in Danger: General Maurice Gamelin and the Politics of French Defence*, Cambridge UP, Cambridge, 1992.
42   Bell, P. M. H., *Origins of the Second World War in Europe*, new edn, Longman, London, 1997.
43   Corum, J. S., *The Roots of Blitzkrieg: Hans von Seeckt and German Military Reform*, Kansas UP, Lawrence, KS, 1992.
44   Doughty, R. S., *The Seeds of Disaster: The Development of French Army Doctrine, 1919–1939*, Archon, Hamden, CT, 1985.
45   Institute for Military History (eds), *Germany and the Second World War, Vol. I: The Build-up of German Aggression*, Clarendon, Oxford, 1990.
46   Martel, G. (ed.), *The Origins of the Second World War Reconsidered: The A. J. P. Taylor Debate after Twenty-Five Years*, Boston, Allen and Unwin, 1986.
47   Millett, A. R. and W. Murray (eds), *Military Effectiveness, Vol. II: The Interwar Period*, Unwin Hyman, Boston,1988.
48   Mommsen, W. and L. Kettenacker (eds), *The Fascist Challenge and the Policy of Appeasement*, Allen and Unwin, London, 1983.
49   Overy, R. J., *The Origins of the Second World War*, 2nd edn, Longman, London, 1998.
50   Parker, R. A. C., *Chamberlain and Appeasement: British Policy and the Coming of the Second World War*, St Martin's, New York, 1993.
51   Post, G., *Dilemmas of Appeasement: British Deterrence and Defense, 1934–1937*, Cornell UP, Ithaca, NY, 1993.
52   Roberts, G., *The Soviet Union and the Origins of the Second World War: Russo-German Relations and the Road to War, 1933–1941*, St Martin's, New York, 1995.
53   Sweet, J. T. T., *Iron Arm: The Mechanization of Mussolini's Army, 1920–1940*, Greenwood, Westport, CT, 1980.
54   Watt, D. C., *How War Came: The Immediate Origins of the Second World War*, Heinemann, London, 1989.
55   Weinberg, G., *The Foreign Policy of Hitler's Germany: Starting World War II*, Chicago UP, Chicago, 1980.

56　Young, R. S., *France and the Origins of the Second World War*, St Martin's, New York, 1996.

CAMPAIGNS EAST AND WEST, 1939–40

57　Bond, B., *Britain, France, Belgium, 1939–1940*, rev edn, Brassey's, London, 1990.
58　Doughty, R. A., *The Breaking Point: Sedan and the Fall of France, 1940*, Archon Books, Hamden, CT, 1990.
59　Gates, E. M., *End of the Affair: The Collapse of the Anglo-French Alliance, 1939–40*, Allen and Unwin, London, 1981.
60　Hough, R. and D. Richards, *The Battle of Britain*, Hodder and Stoughton, London, 1989.
61　Kersaudy, F., *Norway 1940*, Collins, London, 1991.
62　Knox, M., *Mussolini Unleashed, 1939–1941: Politics and Strategy in Italy's Last War*, Cambridge UP, Cambridge, 1982.
63　Paananen, E. and L. Paananen, *The Winter War: The Russo-Finnish Conflict, 1939–1940*, Sidgwick and Jackson, London, 1985.
64　Shirer, W. L., *The Collapse of the Third Republic*, Simon and Schuster, New York, 1969.
65　Zaloga, S. and V. Madej, *The Polish Campaign, 1939*, Hipocrene, New York, 1991.

STRATEGIES FOR SURVIVAL AND EXPANSION, 1940–41

66　Carver, M., *Dilemmas of the Desert War: A New Look at the Libyan Campaign, 1940–1942*, Indiana UP, Bloomington, IN, 1986.
67　Dobson, A. P., *U.S. Wartime Aid to Britain*, St Martin's, New York, 1986.
68　Macdonald, C., *The Lost Battle: Crete 1941*, Free Press, New York, 1993.
69　Research Institute for Military History (eds), *Germany and the Second World War, Vol. III: The Mediterranean, South-East Europe, and North Africa 1939–1941*, Oxford UP, Oxford, 1995.
70　Reynolds, D., *The Creation of the Anglo-American Alliance, 1937–1941: A Study in Competitive Co-operation*, Duke UP, Chapel Hill, NC, 1982.
71　Sainsbury, K., *Churchill and Roosevelt at War*, New York UP, New York, 1994.
72　Van Creveld, M., *Hitler's Strategy, 1940–41: The Balkan Clue*, Cambridge UP, London, 1973.

THE LIMITS OF *BLITZKRIEG*, 1941–42

73　Erickson, J., *The Road to Stalingrad*, Weidenfeld and Nicolson, London, 1975.

74   Glanz, D. M. and J. House, *When Titans Clashed: The Red Army and the Wehrmacht, 1941–1945*, Kansas UP, Lawrence, KA, 1995.
75   Heinrichs, W., *Threshold of War: Franklin D. Roosevelt and American Entry into World War II*, New York UP, New York, 1988.
76   Reinhardt, K., *Moscow – The Turning Point: The Failure of Hitler's Strategy in the Winter of 1941–42*, Berg, Oxford, 1992.
77   Stolfi, R. H. S., *Hitler's Panzers East: World War II Reinterpreted*, Oklahoma UP, Norman, OK, 1991.

ECONOMIES AND SOCIETIES

78   Addison, P., *The Road to 1945: British Politics and the Second World War*, new edn, Pimlico, London, 1993.
79   Anderson, K., *Wartime Women: Sex Roles, Family Relations, and the Status of Women during World War II*, Greenwood, Westport, CT, 1981.
80   Barber, J. and M. Harrison, *The Soviet Home Front: A Social and Economic History of the USSR in World War II*, Longman, London, 1991.
81   Barnett, C., *The Audit of War: The Illusion and Reality of Britain as a Great Nation*, Macmillan, London, 1986.
82   Calder, A., *The People's War: Britain, 1939–1945*, Collins, London, 1969.
83   Calder, A., *The Myth of the Blitz*, Cape, London, 1991.
84   Cairncross, A., *Planning in Wartime: Aircraft Production in Britain, Germany, and the United States*, Macmillan, London, 1991.
85   Chafe, W. H., *The American Woman: Her Changing Social, Economic, and Political Roles, 1920–1970*, Oxford UP, New York, 1972.
86   Garrard, J. (ed.), *World War 2 and the Soviet People*, St Martin's, London, 1993.
87   Herzstein, R., *The War that Hitler Won: Goebbels and the Nazi News Media Campaign*, Paragon, New York, 1987.
88   Jeffreys, K., *The Churchill Coalition and Wartime Politics*, St Martin's, New York, 1995.
89   Koonz, C., *Mothers in the Fatherland: Women, the Family and Nazi Politics*, St Martin's, New York, 1987.
90   Linz, S. J., *The Impact of World War II on the Soviet Union*, Rowman and Allanheld, Totowa, NJ, 1985.
91   Marwick, A. (ed.), *Total War and Social Change*, St Martin's, London, 1988.
92   Milward, A. S., *War, Economy and Society, 1939–1945*, California UP, Berkeley, 1977.
93   Mills, G. T. and H. Rockoff (eds), *The Sinews of War: Essays on the Economic History of World War II*, Iowa UP, Ames, IA, 1993.
94   Noakes, J. (ed.), *The Civilian in War: The Home Front in Europe, Japan and the U.S.A. in World War II*, Exeter UP, Exeter, 1992.

95   Overy, R., *War and Economy in the Third Reich*, Oxford UP, Oxford, 1994.
96   Polenberg, R., *War and Society: The United States, 1941–1945*, Lippincott, Philadelphia, 1972.
97   Reynolds, D., W. F. Kimball, A. O. Chubarian (eds), *Allies at War: The Soviet, American, and British Experience, 1939–1945*, St Martin's, New York, 1994.
98   Summerfield, P., *Women Workers in the Second World War: Production and Patriarchy in Conflict*, Croom Helm, London, 1984.
99   Vatter, H., *The U.S. Economy in World War II*, Columbia UP, New York, 1985.

TECHNOLOGY AND INTELLIGENCE

100   Citino, R. M., *Armored Forces*, Greenwood, Westport, CT, 1994.
101   Deveraux, T. *Messenger Gods of Battle: Radio, Radar, Sonar,* Brassey's, London, 1990.
102   Glanz, D. M., *The Role of Intelligence in Soviet Military Strategy in World War II*, Presidio, Novato, CA, 1990.
103   Hinsley, F. H. and A. Stripp (eds), *Codebreakers: The Inside Story of Bletchly Park*, Oxford UP, Oxford, 1993.
104   Hinsley, F. H., *British Intelligence in the Second World War*, abridged edn, Cambridge UP, Cambridge, 1993.
105   Spence, P. R., *Scientific Information in Wartime: The Allied-German Rivalry, 1939–1945*, Greenwood, Westport, CT, 1994.

BARBARISM AND THE HOLOCAUST

106   Bartov, O., *Hitler's Army: Soldiers, Nazis, and War in the Third Reich*, Oxford UP, New York, 1991.
107   Ibid., *The Eastern Front 1941–45: German Troops and the Barbarization of Warfare*, Macmillan-St Antony's, London, 1985.
108   Browning, C. R., *The Final Solution and the German Foreign Office*, Holmes and Meier, New York, 1978.
109   Finkelstein, N. G., and R. B. Burn, *A Nation on Trial: The Goldhagen Thesis and Historical Truth*, Henry Holt, New York, 1998.
110   Fleming, G., *Hitler and the Final Solution*, California UP, Berkeley, CA, 1984.
111   Gilbert, M., *Auschwitz and the Allies*, Holt, Rhinehart, Winston, New York, 1981.
112   Goldhagen, D. J., *Hitler's Willing Executioners: Ordinary Germans and the Holocaust*, Knopf, New York, 1996.
113   Hilberg, R. (ed.), *The Destruction of the European Jews*, 3 vols, Holmes and Maier, New York, 1984.

114 MacKenzie, S. P., 'The Treatment of Prisoners of War in World War II', *Journal of Modern History*, 66, 1994.

115 Mayer, A., *Why Did the Heavens Not Darken?: The 'Final Solution' in History*, Pantheon, New York, 1988.

116 Rubinstein, W. D., *The Myth of Rescue: Why the democracies could not have saved more Jews from the Nazis*, Routledge, London, 1997.

117 Schulte, T., *The German Army and Nazi Policies in Occupied Russia, 1941–1945*, Berg, Oxford, 1989.

118 Wyman, W., *The Abandonment of the Jews: America and the Holocaust, 1941–1945*, Pantheon, New York, 1984.

COLLABORATION AND RESISTANCE

119 Hawes, S. and R. White (eds), *Resistance in Europe, 1939–1945*, Allen Lane, London, 1975.

120 Hoffmann, P., *The German Resistance to Hitler*, Harvard UP, Cambridge, MA, 1988.

121 Lammers, C. J., 'Levels of Collaboration: A Comparative Study of German Occupation during the Second World War', *Journal of Social Sciences*, 31, 1995.

122 Rings, W., *Life with the Enemy: Collaboration and Resistance in Hitler's Europe, 1939–1945*, Doubleday, New York, 1982.

123 Roberts, W. R., *Tito, Mihailovic and the Allies, 1941–45*, Rutgers UP, New Brunswick, NJ, 1973.

124 Stafford, D., *Britain and European Resistance, 1940–1945*, rev edn, Macmillan-St Antony's, Oxford, 1983.

ALLIANCES AND STRATEGY

125 Butler, G. L., *Second Front Now!*, Macdonald and Janes, London, 1979.

126 Dunn, W. S., *Second Front Now – 1943*, Alabama UP, Montgomery, AL, 1979.

127 Feis, H., *Churchill, Roosevelt, Stalin*, Harper & Row, New York, 1962.

128 Plehwe, F.-K. von, *The End of an Alliance: Rome's defection from the Axis in 1943*, Oxford UP, London, 1971.

129 Sainsbury, K., *The Turning Point*, Oxford UP, Oxford, 1985.

130 Stoler, M., *The Politics of the Second Front*, Greenwood, Westport, CT, 1977.

131 Wilt, A. F., *War From the Top: German and British Decision Making during World War II*, Indiana UP, Bloomington, IN, 1990.

STRATEGIC BOMBING AND THE U-BOAT WAR

132   Crane, C. C., *Bombs, Cities, and Civilians: American Airpower Strategy in World War II*, Kansas UP, Lawrence, KS, 1993.

133   Garrett, S. A., *Ethics and Air Power in World War II: The British Bombing of German Cities*, St Martin's, New York, 1993.

134   Hardesty, V., *The Red Phoenix: The Rise of Soviet Air Power, 1941–1945*, Smithsonian, Washington, DC, 1982.

135   Hastings, M., *Bomber Command*, Dial, New York, 1979.

136   Howarth, S. and D. Law (eds), *The Battle of the Atlantic, 1939–1945*, Greenhill, London, 1994.

137   Mierzejewski, A. C., *The Collapse of the German War Economy, 1944–1945: Allied Air Power and the German National Railway*, North Carolina UP, Chapel Hill, 1988.

138   Milner, M., *The U-Boat Hunters: The Royal Canadian Navy and the offensive against Germany's submarines*, Naval Institute Press, Annapolis, MD, 1994.

139   Milner, M., *North Atlantic Run: The Royal Canadian Navy and the Battle of the Convoys*, Toronto UP, Toronto, 1985.

140   Murray, W., *Strategy for Defeat: The Luftwaffe, 1933–1945*, Chartwell, Secaucus, NJ, 1985.

141   Richards, D., *The Hardest Victory: RAF Bomber Command in the Second World War*, Norton, London, 1994.

142   Runyan, T. J. and J. M. Copes (eds), *To Die Gallantly: The Battle of the Atlantic*, Westview, Boulder, CO, 1994.

143   Shaffer, R., *Wings of Judgment: American Bombing in World War II*, Oxford UP, New York, 1985.

144   Syrett, D., *The Defeat of the German U-Boats: The Battle of the Atlantic*, South Carolina UP, Columbia, SC, 1994.

145   Terraine, J., *The Right of the Line: The Royal Air Force in the European War, 1939–1945*, Hodder and Stoughton, London, 1985.

146   Van Der Vat, D., *The Atlantic Campaign: World War II's Great Struggle at Sea*, Harper and Row, New York, 1988.

THE CHANGING BALANCE OF FORTUNE, 1942-43

147   Barnett, C., *The Desert Generals*, rev edn, Indiana UP, Bloomington, IN, 1986.

148   D'Este, C., *World War II in the Mediterranean, 1942–1945*, Algonquin, Chapel Hill, NC, 1990.

149   Gelb, N., *Desperate Venture: The Story of Operation Torch*, Murrow, New York, 1992.

150   Glanz, D. M., *From the Don to the Dnepr: Soviet Offensive Operations, December 1942–August 1943*, Frank Cass, London, 1991.

151   Ziemke, E. F. and M. E. Bauer, *Moscow to Stalingrad: Decision in the East*, US Army Center of Military History, Washington, DC, 1987.

SUCCESS AND FAILURE SOUTH AND EAST, 1943–44

152   D'Este, C., *Fatal Decision: Anzio and the Battle for Rome*, HarperCollins, New York, 1991.

153   Ibid., *Bitter Victory: The Battle for Sicily, July–August 1943*, Dutton, New York, 1988.

154   Erickson, J., *The Road to Berlin*, Westview, Boulder, CO, 1983.

155   Graham, D. and S. Bidwell, *Tug of War: The Battle for Italy, 1943–1945*, St Martin's, New York, 1986.

156   Wray, T. A., *Standing Fast: German Defensive Doctrine on the Russian Front during World War II*, Combat Studies Institute, Fort Leavenworth, KS, 1986.

CLOSING THE RING, 1944–45

157   D'Este, C., *Decision in Normandy*, Dutton, New York, 1983.

158   Duffy, C., *Red Storm over the Reich*, Atheneum, New York, 1991.

159   English, J. A., *The Canadian Army in the Normandy Campaign*, Praeger, Westport, CT, 1981.

160   Le Tissier, T., *Zhukov on the Oder: The Decisive Battle for Berlin*, Praeger, Westport, CT, 1996.

161   Neipold, G., *Battle for White Russia: The Destruction of Army Group Centre, June 1944*, Brassey's, London, 1987.

162   Patrick Murray, G. E., *Eisenhower versus Montgomery: The Continuing Debate*, Praeger, Westport, CT, 1996.

163   Weighley, R. F., *Eisenhower's Lieutenants: The Campaign of France and Germany, 1944–1945*, Indiana UP, Bloomington, IN, 1981.

EUROPE DIVIDED

164   Douglas, R., *From War to Cold War, 1942–1948*, Macmillan, London, 1981.

165   McCauley, M., *Origins of the Cold War*, Longman, London, 1983.

166   Thomas, H., *Armed Truce: The Beginnings of the Cold War, 1945–1946*, Atheneum, New York, 1987.

WINNING AND LOSING

167   Addison, P. and A. Calder (eds), *Time to Kill: The Soldier's Experience of War in the West, 1939–45*, Pimlico, London, 1977.

168   Doubler, M. D., *Closing with the Enemy: How GIs Fought the War in Europe, 1944–1945*, Kansas UP, Lawrence, KS, 1994.

169   Ellis, J., *Brute Force: Allied Strategy and Tactics in the Second World War*, Viking, New York, 1990.

170   Fraser, D., *And We Shall Shock Them: The British Army in the Second World War*, Hodder and Stoughton, London, 1983.

171   Fritz, S. G., *Frontsoldaten: The German Soldier in World War II*,
       Kentucky UP, Lexington, KY, 1995.
172   Millett, A. R. and W. Murray (eds), *Military Effectiveness, Vol. III:*
       The Second World War, Unwin Hyman, Boston, 1988.
173   Overy, R. J., *Why the Allies Won*, Norton, New York, 1996.
174   Van Creveld, M., *Fighting Power: German and US Army Performance,*
       1939–1945, Greenwood, Westport, CT, 1982.

INDEX